CANADIAN GOLD
2002

A FENN PUBLISHING BOOK

FENN PUBLISHING COMPANY LTD.
Bolton, Canada

Distributed in Canada by H.B. Fenn and Company Ltd.
Bolton, Ontario, Canada L7E 1W2

Officially licensed by the International Ice Hockey Federation (IIHF)
and Hockey Hall of Fame (HHOF)

National Library of Canada Cataloguing in Publication Data

PODNIEKS, ANDREW
CANADIAN GOLD 2002

ISBN 1-55168-268-0

1. Olympic Winter Games (19th : 2002 : Salt Lake City, Utah)
2. Hockey—Canada—History—21st century. I. Title.

GV848.4.C3P64 2002   796.962'66   C2002-901192-2

Printed and bound in Canada

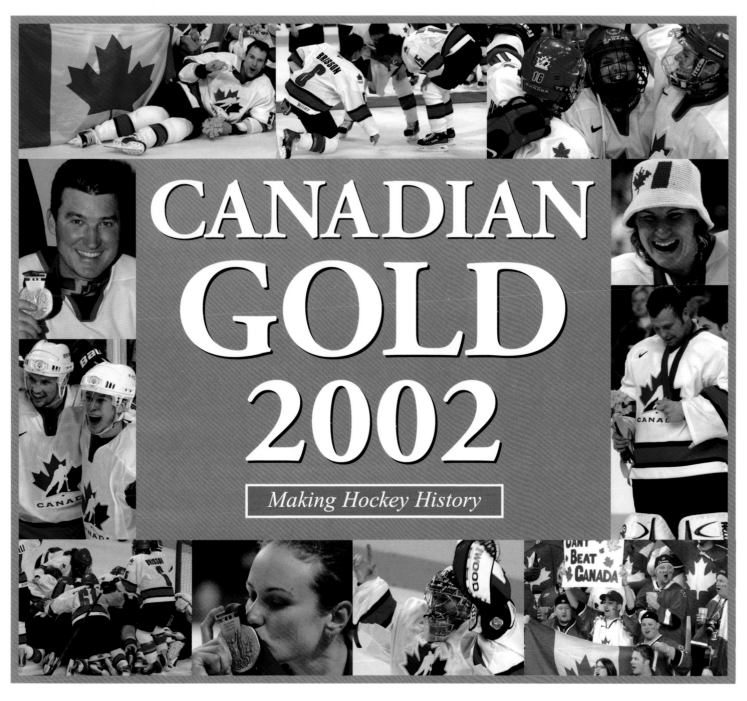

CANADIAN GOLD 2002

Making Hockey History

ANDREW PODNIEKS

Fenn Publishing Company Ltd

CONTENTS

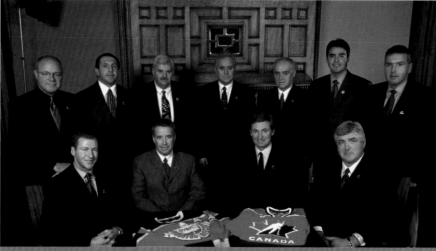

The executive for the men's Canadian Olympic hockey team, Salt Lake City 2002

(opposite, top) Wayne Gretzky flanked by Lowe (back left) and CHA president Bob Nicholson (right).

(opposite, bottom) Assistant coach Jacques Martin (left), Assistant coach Ken Hitchcock (middle), Head coach Pat Quinn (right).

INTRODUCTION

It's difficult to say which story is the greater, which the more compelling or meaningful. The answer is, likely, both. Canada's men's hockey team won gold for the first time in fifty years—fifty years to the day, no less!—and the women won gold after an exhibition season which seemed, if not doomed, then on course for silver, not gold.

In their own ways, both stories of triumph began with the executives, the people who put the teams together and coached the teams to victory. Wayne Gretzky's success was, in itself, improbable. He became general manager of the team without having had a single day's experience at the job for which he was hired. But, in his case, a great player became a great manager, and he was smart enough to surround himself with exceptional people. Coach Pat Quinn made a dramatic contribution to the team long before the opening faceoff against Sweden. "Back in September," he recounted after victory, "one of the things we did was address problems that came out of Nagano, and many of the players told us the biggest thing for them was the fear factor, the fear of losing and how to deal with it." For Bob Nicholson, head of Canadian Hockey, his solution was to go with the best and be faithful to

them. In the end, they all did their job to perfection.

For women's coach Daniele Sauvageau, the problems weren't much different. She coached the team through a rough series of eight losses to the Americans in the months leading up to Salt Lake and then made a bold change in roster, cutting Nancy Drolet and inserting Cherie Piper. If Sauvageau had failed, it might have cost her her job. Instead, it proved to be a touch of genius to a roster that had become, perhaps, complacent.

In both cases, the men and women arrived in Salt Lake with curious public emotion behind them. Canadians expected their teams to win, in the sense that they wanted victory so much that nothing else would suffice. Yet, truly, no one in the country could have expected both teams to come away with gold. Paradoxically, then, the country's high expectations were exceeded by the players.

As I sat waiting for the men's finals to start, I was consumed by the weight of history being dumped onto the ice at the E-Center. Anyone in Canada who thinks of hockey victory thinks of two moments—Henderson's goal in 1972, and Mario's in '87. What both goals had in common was late drama, and as I sat

in the press tribune on the February 24, I felt almost sick thinking about such an ending to this game. You want that kind of ending, you pray to be witness to such a tremendous moment, but the thought of having to endure 59 minutes of gut-wrenching hockey to get there was overwhelming. Better to go up 5-0 and coast to a victory, I thought. Forget the drama. Let's win and get out of here.

Victory was not last minute. The drama came not from late-game heroics but in preserving a lead and defending to the death. The women held off a late surge by the American women to win 3-2, and the men clung to a one- and then two-goal lead until a late, brilliant shot by Joe Sakic sealed the win with under two minutes to go.

That both wins came at the expense of the United States added another very meaningful layer of glory to the double-gold sweep. The U.S. is bigger, politically stronger, and militarily more powerful, but we are still capable of sending our neighbours to the south a clear message: you can try to meddle with our fish or lumber or border regulations, you can steal our doctors and pillage our water, but don't ever, ever try to take away our hockey—you can't, and you won't. It's our game—forever. 🍁

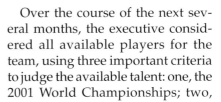

Bob Nicholson, president of the Canadian Hockey Association, changed the course of Canada's National Team on November 8, 2000 when he hired the great Wayne Gretzky as executive director of hockey operations for Salt Lake City 2002. It was a move predicated by Gretzky's love of his country and the game he played so very well. He was hired well ahead of the Olympics in order that he might first oversee the country's entry in the 2001 World Championships and work with his staff over a period of time leading up to Salt Lake.

Coach Pat Quinn and assistants Wayne Fleming and Kevin Lowe were also hired on November 8, 2000. A short time later, Ken Hitchcock and Jacques Martin were added to the coaching staff. As a

group, the first job for these men was to name eight players to Canada's Olympic team by March 23, 2001, a job made all the easier by the return of Mario Lemieux just a few months earlier. The Magnificent One was named captain on that Super Eight day.

Over the course of the next several months, the executive considered all available players for the team, using three important criteria to judge the available talent: one, the 2001 World Championships; two, the brief training camp in Calgary, Alberta prior to the opening of NHL camps in September 2001; three, the first part of the NHL season. They had fixed December 22, 2001 as the date to name the remaining players, but that was moved up a week. On December 15, 2001, Nicholson, Gretzky, Quinn, Lowe, and everyone else at Canadian Hockey held a special news conference at the Hockey Hall of Fame in Toronto to name the final 15 players, a list that did not change by even one name in the coming weeks. It was a gold medal list. ✹

WOMEN'S EXECUTIVE

The executive of Canada's women's team consists of head coach Daniele Sauvageau and assistants Melody Davidson and Wally Kozak. Sauvageau was hired on June 22, 2000 to coach the Olympic team, though she was the obvious choice after leading Canada to a fifth consecutive World Championships gold in 1999 and later a seventh win in 2001.

She began as an assistant in 1996, first with the national under-19 team and then with the World Championship team. She remained an assistant through the silver medal performance at Nagano and shortly after became head coach. She also was hired as an assistant for the Montreal Rocket of the QMJHL for 1999-2000,

the first woman to coach in major junior hockey.

Melody Davidson was hired as Sauvageau's assistant on the same day, June 22, 2000, after having been an assistant to the gold medal team that won the 2001 World Championships in Minnesota. She had been the head coach for the 2000 champions, and her career began back in 1994 as an assistant at that year's Worlds. Additionally, Davidson

coached Connecticut College for three years (1997-2000).

Wally Kozak goes back a long way, to the 1968-69 season when he played for Canada's National Team. He later played in the IHL before embarking on a lengthy coaching career. He was variously coach of men's teams that won gold, silver, and bronze in the Spengler Cup, and has also bossed the bench in the Provincial Junior league in Alberta, the CIAU, and the WHL. Kozak coached in Japan for four years (1994-1998) and more recently with the Oval X-Treme women's team that won the 2001 Esso Women's National Hockey Championships. He served as an assistant at both the 2000 and 2001 World Championships. ❧

DAY 1

February 9   **Men**
GERMANY 3   **SLOVAKIA 0**
4 p.m.   **E-Center**

Germany conjured up haunting memories of the past by stunning Slovakia 3-0 on opening day, with goals from Jurgen Rumrich, Jan Benda, and Klaus Kathan. Goaltender Marc Seliger made 29 saves —many terrific—to earn the shutout. The result recalled Slovakia's 4-2 loss to Germany on February 12, 1998, which put the undermanned squad in 10th place at the Nagano Olympics. In the 2002 rematch, the Slovaks used just 16 skaters (ten forwards, six defence-men). They used NHL scoring ace Zigmund Palffy even though he was only supposed to sit and watch from the bench, according to GM Peter Stastny's agreement with the Los Angeles Kings. But Palffy couldn't get much done as the pro-Slovak crowd chanted desperately, "Please get a goal! Please get a goal!" Rumrich scored a short-handed goal early in the second, and Benda scored on the power play six and a half minutes later. Kathan added an empty-netter at 19:07 of the third with Pavol Rybar on the bench for an extra attacker. ❦

February 9   **Men**
BELARUS 1   **UKRAINE 0**
2 p.m.   **The Peaks**

In the opening game of the 2002 Olympic hockey tournament, Belarus enjoyed a solid performance from goaltender Sergei Shabanov, who posted the shutout with 17 saves in a surprising 1-0 Belarus win. Oleg Mikulchik, a veteran defenseman with NHL and North American minor pro experience, scored the winning goal midway through the third period. Thirty shots on goal was a high number for Belarus, a team that often suffered from holding the puck too long. It was a welcome start to the tournament for the Belarussians, who were demoted from the elite group at the 2001 IIHF World Championships and faced the prospect of having to re-qualify in 2002. This was a chippy game with 32 total minutes in penalties, high by international standards. Ukraine's many goalie changes in the dying moments didn't pay off with the tying goal.

February 9 **Men**
LATVIA 4 **AUSTRIA 2**
7 p.m. **The Peaks**

The superior skill of Team Latvia was too much for Austria to handle in this preliminary round game. The Austrians battled back from a 2-0 deficit to tie the score early in the second period on Matthias Trattnig's unassisted goal. But less than four minutes later, Gregorijs Pantelejevs scored the eventual game winner. Veteran forward Harijs Vitolins led Latvia with a goal and an assist, while Leonids Tambijevs had two helpers. Vyacheslavs Fanduls and Igors Bondarevs also scored for Latvia, while the gifted youngster Oliver Setzinger had a goal for Austria. This outcome appeared to set the typical tone for Austria: always near the bottom of the international hockey battle, but hard-working and well-coached enough to keep the score close. Reinhard Divis, one of the American Hockey League's top netminders, wasn't particularly sharp in this opener, though, stopping just 15 out of the 19 shots he faced. Sergejs Naumovs of Latvia, who earned his living with Djurgarden of the Swedish League, did better with 26 saves.

February 9 **Men**
Switzerland 3 **France 3**
9 p.m. **E-Center**

After shutting out the Minnesota Wild on Friday night in an NHL game for his Colorado Avalanche, David Aebischer provided his Swiss National Team with a sub-par performance in its first game of the Olympics, a 3-3 tie with France on Saturday night.

His uneven play might well be attributed to his hectic schedule in the previous 24 hours. After the Colorado game, he checked into a Denver hotel near the airport at around midnight, got a few hours' sleep before his 7 a.m. flight, and practised with his Swiss National team in the morning before getting some food and sleep.

"I could have played better than I played tonight," he admitted, "but we got a point and they're a pretty good team." In truth, Aebischer had only a few good chances against over the first 40 minutes and France scored on a rebound on a five-on-three and a beautiful converted pass on a two-on-one rush.

In the third, though, he made a number of terrific saves, including two in the first minute with his team down a man. The Swiss scored just

a few minutes later to tie the game 2-2, but France went ahead midway through after a number of close-in chances. "I think I should have had that," Aebischer said. "I lifted my pad a bit, and it went in." Still, he stopped Philippe Bozon on a partial breakaway midway through the game and slid across the crease to block a one-timer from the point on another French power play.

The most difficult part of Aebischer's transition from NHLer to Olympian overnight was not getting to know his teammates. "I know almost everybody, maybe one or two players I didn't know. It wasn't a problem to play with them right away. I felt comfortable in this situation."

Instead, it was the rules that had him most confused. "For instance," he explained, "with the offside rule, I got caught once or twice thinking it was offside and it wasn't, so that's the biggest change for me."

DAY 2

February 10   Men
GERMANY 3   AUSTRIA 2
4 p.m.   The Peaks

Andreas Loth scored with just 1:14 left in the third period to give Germany a dramatic 3-2 win over neighbouring Austria in their second game of the preliminary round of the 2K2 Olympics. The win at the Provo City/Utah County Ice Arena at Seven Peaks improved their record to 2-0 and assured the Germans control of their own destiny in the three-game round-robin.

For the second straight game, the Austrians fell behind 2-0, rallied to tie, and ended up losing. Today, they deserved a better fate. Although the Germans were decidedly the best team over the first 20 minutes, the red-sweatered Austrians controlled the rest of the game, scoring two to tie in the second, and outshooting the Germans 16-4 in the third (31-22 overall), though Loth was the only goal scorer of the final period. "We knew they were going to come out strong, even after their game yesterday. They're not going to give up; they dump the puck in and pressure a lot. In the second period, they put us under pressure body-wise," said Jan Benda.

The reliable play of Marc Seliger in goal has been the story on ice so far at these Olympics and eased the Germans' worry over the injury to Olaf Kolzig which prevented the Washington Capitals goalie from joining the Salt Lake team. "We didn't know if we'd get anybody at all," Mark MacKay explained.

February 10   Men
LATVIA 6   SLOVAKIA 6
7 p.m.   E-Center

At the start of Latvia's second preliminary round game with Slovakia, the story was the unavailability of goalie Arturs Irbe. By the end of this crazy 6-6 tie, it almost didn't matter who appeared between the pipes for either team. The result killed Slovakia's chances of moving on to the final round. Aleksandrs Macijevskis scored a pair of goals to pace Latvia and Sandis Ozolinsh earned four assists in his lone Olympic appearance. Slovak stars, including Josef Stumpel, Pavol Demitra, and Marian Hossa, also scored, but their team blew a 6-3 lead heading into the third period as a result of its weak defensive play. Team Latvia head coach Curt Lindstrom praised the work of goaltender Sergejs Naumovs, who faced 35 shots, going so far as to speculate about how many kisses Naumovs might get from the President of Latvia for this performance! In a controversial move, Slovak head coach Jan Filc scratched defenseman Zdeno Chara of the Ottawa Senators from the lineup to keep a roster spot open for Peter Bondra. Filc said afterward that he would likely lose his job due to Slovakia's failure to advance to the final round. ♣

Austria's Dieter Kalt (left) has his sweater hooked by Germany's Jan Benda in action at the Peaks during Day 2 of the Games.

DAY 3

CANADA 7
KAZAKHSTSAN 0

February 11   Women
11:05 a.m.   E-Center

When Kazakhstan fell 7-0 to Canada in the first game of the women's Olympic hockey tournament, it improved on its one previous meeting with the Canadians at the 2001 World Championships in Minneapolis, an 11-0 loss. This match marked Kazakhstan's Olympic debut in women's hockey. Hayley Wickenheiser and Vicky Sunohara led the offensive assault for Canada

"A lot has changed since 1998. Having been to one Oylmpics, having the experience and a taste of what it's like is so valuable."
JENNIFER BOTTERILL

with two goals apiece, while Danielle Goyette notched a goal and two assists.

Tammy Lee Shewchuk's tally was the prettiest of the game, as she took a long pass and broke between the Kazakh defense to score five-hole on beleaguered netminder Natalya Trunova at 3:49 of the second period. "I can't imagine another place I'd rather be right now," Shewchuk said. "We have such a great group of girls on this team. They're a lot of fun, very passionate and very committed. As for Kazakhstan, they seem to be improving every year. They're definitely stronger than they were last year. Their goalie played one heck of a game. You have to take your hat off to her. She does hit the ice quite early and we had to adjust ourselves to get the rebounds up high."

GAME SUMMARY

First Period

1	Canada, Wickenheiser (unassisted)	2:33
2	Canada, Piper (Antal, Sostorics)	8:45
3	Canada, Sunohara (Piper, Ouellette)	11:09

penalties: Taikevich (Kaz) 2:30
Botterill (Can) 3:51
Khlyzova (Kaz) 9:20
Campbell (Can) 19:25

Second Period

4	Canada, Shewchuk (Goyette, Sostorics)	3:49
5	Canada, Wickenheiser (Goyette)	15:18

penalties: Brisson (Can) 1:37
Taikevich (Kaz) 3:04
Taikevich (Kaz) 5:10
Taikevich (Kaz) 9:14
(Kaz-delay of game) 14:16
Shtelmaister (Kaz) 17:02
Potapova (Kaz) 20:00

Third Period

6	Canada, Goyette (Wickenheiser)	7:27
7	Canada, Sunohara (Hefford)	17:23

penalties: Solovyeva (Kaz) 6:57
Ouellette (Can) 8:23

In Goal

CANADA Kim St. Pierre
KAZAKHSTAN Natalya Trunova

Shots on Goal

CANADA	24	18	24	66
KAZAKHSTAN	3	3	5	11

Referee Anne Haanpaa
Linesmen Tina Kirschner/Megan Mackenzie

"We started up a bit slow but by the third period we picked it up and their goalie played quite well."

"We're coming in as a little bit as the underdogs. Having had one Olympics under our belts, we're pretty relaxed and we know what we have to do to be successful."
HAYLEY WICKENHEISER

Physically, Kazakhstan was outmatched. To illustrate the problem, the team had the shortest player in this tournament in Svetlana Vassina (4'11½") and the lightest in Lyubov Alexeyeva (99 pounds). That took its toll in one-on-one battles and along the boards. The Kazakhs showed ability in skating and passing, but they were prone to puckhandling errors and fired weak shots. They recorded only eleven shots in the game to Canada's 66.

"We hope we will meet Team Canada again and play better next time," said Kazakh blueliner

"It's been a month since we played the Americans. Both sides know it's going to be a great game and we'll see what happens."
DANIELE SAUVAGEAU

Oxsana Taikevich. "For us, it was a good first game," said Team Canada head coach Daniele Sauvageau. "In the third period, we played with a little bit more poise and moved the puck very well. We need to make sure that we're doing what we're supposed to as a team." At this early stage, it looked like a good first step along the road to gold for Canada at Salt Lake.

"The Americans are a great team and the competition pushes you to be better. They've raised the bar. It's always a great game between our two teams."
THERESE BRISSON

"We are definitely building towards the U.S. game, but we can't overlook other teams. It's building blocks right now and we need to improve each and every shift."
CHERYL POUNDER

"Usually, games like that are tough, but the crowd was amazing. I just kept reminding myself that I was at the Olympics. I was going to enjoy every second of it."
KIM ST. PIERRE

February 11   Men
UKRAINE 5   SWITZERLAND 2
4 p.m.   E-Center

Coach Ralph Krueger expected so much more for his Swiss team during these Olympics, but after today's 5-2 loss to the Ukraine his team will not advance to the medal round beginning this Friday. "We've got to go home and figure out what the hell happened," he said afterward.

In the Ukraine dressing room, the mood was ebullient. After playing a lacklustre game to open the tournament—a 1-0 loss to Belarus—the team came out with much more enthusiasm today at the E-Center.

Their best effort was augmented by the addition of Ruslan Fedotenko from the Philadelphia Flyers and Sergei Varlamov of the St. Louis Blues, both of whom scored for the Ukraine.

The Ukraine scored just 2:08 into the game. Swiss forward Martin Steinegger made a great rush into the Ukraine zone and was hooked to the ice. No call was made by referee Kevin Acheson, and the Ukes came right back with a long shot that David Aebischer kicked out weakly to Valentyn Oletsky, who scored.

The teams each scored before the end of the period, but an early goal against Aebischer 1:19 into the second moved Kreuger to pull the NHL goalie in favour of Martin Gerber.

"We came out for the game tonight more prepared than the opening game," Toronto Maple Leafs forward Alexei Ponikarovsky said after being released by the team from the farm in St. John's, Newfoundland to play. "I think our line, with Fedotenkov, Varlamov, we maybe added some freshness to the game."

The win gave the Ukraine two points in Group B, and the team will play its final game of the round robin on Wednesday against France at the Peaks. Although the Ukrainians won't have Varlamov in the lineup (he'll be back in the NHL, according to coach Bogdanov) they will have Dmitri Khristich of the Washington Capitals.   ♦

February 11   Women
SWEDEN 3   RUSSIA 2
2 p.m.   The Peaks

Sweden eked out a 3-2 win over Russia in its women's opener despite outshooting its weaker opponent 44-14. The Swedes got goals from Ann-Louise Edstrand, Lotta Almblad, and Kristina Bergstrand to open a 3-0 lead by 4:11 of the second period. But Russia's top forward, Ekaterina Pachkevitch, got her team on the board less than a minute later, and Larisa Mishina made it 3-2 at 16:04. Russia's aggressive play earned five minor penalties compared to just two for Sweden. At this early stage of the Olympics, the results seemed to indicate that both teams would be hard pressed to outdo Finland for a bronze medal behind Canada and the United States.

February 11   Men
BELARUS 3   FRANCE 1
7 p.m.   The Peaks

With a 3-1 loss to Belarus, France failed to build on the momentum of its surprising 3-3 tie with Switzerland in its opener, despite outshooting the Belarussians 23-21. The French got off to a nice start when three-time French League MVP Maurice Rozenthal converted a setup from ex-St. Louis Blues forward Philippe Bozon at 3:31 of the first period. But Andrei Rassolko tied the score less than five minutes later, and in the second, another former NHLer, Vladimir Tsyplakov, got the winning goal with assists to power play point men Oleg Romanov and Oleg Khmyl, the latter being the all-time points leader among Belarus defencemen. Pankov added an insurance score with just over two minutes left in the third and France could muster no greater offense when it pulled goalie Cristobal Huet in the final minute of play. Earlier in the game, at 8:28 of the second, Huet stopped Andrei Kovalev on a penalty shot (see photos), the only one of these 2002 Olympics. ◆

DAY 4

February 12   **Women**
USA 10   **GERMANY 0**
11 a.m.   **E-Center**

At the 4:39 mark of the first period, Germany registered its second shot on goal, the same number as the United States. It was all downhill from there for the country competing in women's hockey for the first time at the Olympics. The USA whitewashed Germany 10-0. Karyn Bye led the points parade with four (two goals and two assists), and Julie Chu had one and one.

Germany did not register its third shot until 16:53 of the period, and in the second had two more by default: one came from centre ice, and the other from in front of its own goal, which would have been icing had the puck been off target. In fact, Germany would have been credited with more than the five icings they committed during the game (the same number as the United States) save for the fact that the players were quite literally not strong enough to propel the puck down the ice with enough speed or force for it to cross the red line. In all, the shots were 57-8. Even if Germany scored on all its shots... well, do the math.

"We prepared well and had a lot of confidence coming into this game," Chu said with diplomacy.

"Our first period was very good, but we have to go home and work step by step, practise more, get more girls to play," Sabine Ruckauer said of her country's game and, by ex-tension, national program. Indeed, the Americans started off with a little nervous hitch in their git-along, but when they came out for the second their nerves had been replaced by exuberance. They chased Stephanie Wartosch-Kurten from the German net after the sixth goal — though she had played extremely well to that point — and didn't allow a single shot inside their blueline for a span of more than 42 minutes. In the second period, the Germans had the puck on their sticks inside the American blueline a total of seven times and about 24 seconds.

One humourous moment occurred at 15:45 of the third when two pucks appeared on the ice during play! At the previous whistle, German goalie Esther Thyssen had lost the puck in her equipment, so referee Laura Vanderhorst (a Winnipeg, Manitoba firefighter by day) got a new puck. When action continued around the goal, the first puck dislodged from Thyssen's equipment, forcing a stop in play .

"The thing I liked most about the game were all the flags," Tara Mounsey noted after the game. "When we stepped out during the warmup to hear the chants of "USA! USA!" was so wonderful," A.J. (Alison) Mleczko agreed.

The USA victory was as impressive as Canada's 7-0 crushing of Kazakhstan and lends further credence to the obvious conclusion to the women's side of the tournament — an all-North American showdown for gold, again.

TEAM CANADA'S FIRST PRESS CONFERENCE—MEN

Team Canada made its presence felt this afternoon at the E-Center in Salt Lake City when general manager Wayne Gretzky and assistant Kevin Lowe held a press conference also attended by one of the team's assistant coaches, Ken Hitchcock.

Lowe affirmed what many Europeans might already feel—that the Dominator's team is still the favourite. "We always say in the National Hockey League that the team that won the previous championship is always the team to beat, so we think the Czechs are the team to beat," he said. "They won the last gold medal and Dominik Hasek is still as dominant as he was back then. I'm sure they think they can win this gold medal as much as the Canadians do. The Czechs, to me, are the team to beat."

Indeed, in addition to winning gold at Nagano, the Czech national team is also the only nation to win medals in each of the last six World Championships. They won gold in 1996, bronze in '97 and '98, and are currently the three-time world champions with golds in 1999, 2000, and 2001. These facts do not deter Gretzky, however.

"The great thing about hockey in our country is that everyone expects us to be the best," he said. "Our focus has been a gold medal from day one." This is a confidence that comes from his trust in Canada's players—and not their health. Al MacInnis is playing through an ankle injury tonight; Steve Yzerman skated hard today and will play Monday night to test a knee that recently underwent arthroscopic surgery; Owen Nolan and Mario Lemieux are just on the happy side of healthy after recovering from recent injuries.

Much as he'd love to step into the lineup, though, Gretzky realizes he can help the team these days only in a jacket and tie. "We all get old one day—that's part of life," he said without sentiment. "There's no question it's harder to watch a game than it is to play; it's a much more stressful situation to watch. When you play and make a mistake, you can go out there on the next shift and do something about it; when you're sitting up top, it's much more difficult."

For assistant coach Ken Hitchcock, the concern is more what happens on ice than in the press conference. Despite much concern in Canada about getting minutes to all the superstars on the team, he sees no disadvantage in turning over four lines all tournament long and giving the leaders 17 minutes a game instead of their usual 25 or 30. "You can't win in this competition without playing four lines," he said without equivocation. "You can't. It's too quick. It's two hour and 15 minute games, the rotation's too quick, there's 15-minute intermissions, the five-second rule is in place for faceoffs. You've got to have four lines. The game's too quick."

And with that, the Team Canada executive completed their first appearance in Salt Lake City and retired to private rooms to strategize for their opening game, February 15, against Sweden. ❧

February 12	Women
FINLAND 4	CHINA 0
2 p.m.	The Peaks

They say your best players have to be your best players if you want to win, and that was certainly the case in Finland's tournament-opening 4-0 victory over China. In front of 4,977 fans, the prolific veteran Riikka Nieminen set up three goals by Karoliina Rantamaki, Katja Riipi, and Emma Laaksonen. Saija Sirvio added some insurance with less than three minutes left in the game. Finnish goalie Tuula Puputti, who plays U.S. college hockey, did what she had to, making 12 mostly routine saves while her teammates fired 54 shots at China's Hong Guo. This was a rematch of the 1998 Olympic women's bronze medal game in which Finland defeated China, 4-1.

FEBRUARY 12

Team Russia announced today that center Pavel Datsyuk of the Detroit Red Wings will replace the injured Viktor Kozlov on its Olympic roster.

The 23-year-old graduate of AK Bars Kazan is enjoying a strong NHL rookie season with nine goals and 15 assists in 52 games. Drafted in the sixth round in 1998, Datsyuk becomes the eleventh Red Wing heading to the 2002 Games.

Austria's Peter Kasper ties up his man, Lubos Bartecko of Slovakia on a day the Slovaks dressed just 13 skaters.

national club player, Jan Pardavy, replying for the Slovaks. A chippy element entered into the last ten minutes of the third period as Pardavy took a ten-minute misconduct for a nasty elbow and Austria's Gunther Lanzinger received the same for checking from behind. Peter Stastny's team had little to play for in this game, since their chances of advancing to the final round had ended. ✦

Austrian goalie Reinhard Divis follows the puck while Slovak captain Robert Petrovicky fights for territory in front.

February 12 Men
SLOVAKIA 3 AUSTRIA 2
4 p.m. E-Center

Slovakia's 3-2 loss to Austria completed the Olympic elimination for this undermanned team, which gambled by keeping roster spots open for NHL stars who never arrived. Simon Wheeldon, a Canadian-born scoring star with the Victoria Cougars in the 1980s, led the way for the Austrians with a goal and an assist. Gerhard Unterluggaeur scored the winner at 9:09 of the third period, and Dieter Kalt added the other Austrian goal. No big-name Slovak NHLers contributed to their side. Instead, it was Rastislav Pavlikovsky, a 1998 ninth-round pick of the Ottawa Senators with minor pro experience, and

February 12   **Men**
GERMANY 4   **LATVIA 1**
7 p.m.   **The Peaks**

German head coach Hans Zach's band of warriors beat a far more talented Latvian squad 4-1 by completely shutting them down with bodychecks, stickwork, and, more generally, irritating behaviour. Yet it was barely controlled mayhem. At the end of the night, the penalty minutes were even at ten apiece. The result assured Germany the Qualifier II spot for the final round starting three days later, while Latvia fell out of contention. Marc Seliger had another good game in goal for Germany, while Arturs Irbe's lone outing with Latvia went for nothing, as the Carolina Hurricanes netminder just wasn't sharp. "Our hopes were shattered by a really good team with a capital T," said Irbe, who was reluctant to concede that the kerfuffle with the NHL about his non-availability for the Latvia-Slovakia game had taken a toll on him mentally. Latvian coach Curt Lindstrom took the loss in stride, pointing out that the country has only 2.5 million people and celebrates wildly when it wins in hockey. And what happens after a loss? "The sun will come up again tomorrow." The Germans finished the preliminary round with a perfect 3-0 record.

DAY 5

CANADA 7
RUSSIA 0

**February 13   Women
11 a.m.   E-Center**

Unfortunately, this was the only Canada-Russia hockey game involving either men or women in Salt Lake City. Since 2002 marked the 30th anniversary of the famous 1972 Summit Series, it might have been tempting to draw comparisons or wax nostalgic over the passage of so much time, but Canada's overwhelming dominance in this women's game laid to rest any analogous possibilities. Hayley Wickenheiser and Danielle

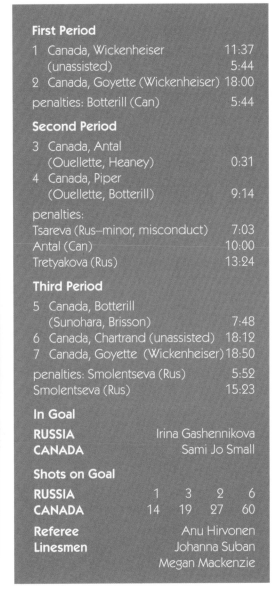

First Period

1 Canada, Wickenheiser		11:37
(unassisted)		5:44
2 Canada, Goyette (Wickenheiser)		18:00
penalties: Botterill (Can)		5:44

Second Period

3 Canada, Antal		
(Ouellette, Heaney)		0:31
4 Canada, Piper		
(Ouellette, Botterill)		9:14
penalties:		
Tsareva (Rus—minor, misconduct)		7:03
Antal (Can)		10:00
Tretyakova (Rus)		13:24

Third Period

5 Canada, Botterill		
(Sunohara, Brisson)		7:48
6 Canada, Chartrand (unassisted)		18:12
7 Canada, Goyette (Wickenheiser)		18:50
penalties: Smolentseva (Rus)		5:52
Smolentseva (Rus)		15:23

In Goal

RUSSIA	Irina Gashennikova
CANADA	Sami Jo Small

Shots on Goal

RUSSIA	1	3	2	6
CANADA	14	19	27	60

Referee	Anu Hirvonen
Linesmen	Johanna Suban
	Megan Mackenzie

*"I think we're behind Canada by one year, if we continue with the kind of training we have had this year.
Until (late August) all of our team members were playing on their respective clubs."*

"The time will come when we'll be able to defeat them occasionally."
VIACHESLAV DOLGUSHIN

Goyette led the way offensively with their multi-point efforts as Canada peppered Russian goalie Irina Gashennikova with 60 shots. "I have a little bit of a headache, but tomorrow I should be fine," Gashennikova quipped afterward. She wasn't the only one in pain. Prior to the Olympics, Canadian television had run humourous beer ads depicting Russian hockey players fearfully reserv-

ing stretchers before their game against Canada. That joke actually fit the bill for this game here because shot-blocking Russian women had to be helped off the ice several times, including Ekaterina Pachkevitch and Elena Bialkovskaia. Overall, the Russians did not display the form that earned them a bronze medal at the 2001 World Championships in Minnesota. "I was surprised

the Russians weren't able to get more shots," said Canadian head coach Daniele Sauvageau. "But on the other hand, we played very well defensively. I give a lot of credit to our team." ✤

"I think we expected a tough and physical game. We got some confidence today, but we still have some jitters."
CASSIE CAMPBELL

"Every game is important. These guys played great and did a lot of great things too. We were going out to play the best we could."

"It's our game, and we feel pressure, mostly from ourselves, to win a gold medal."
DANA ANTAL

"Both of our goalies should be number one. We had decided on the first two games (to alternate goalies), and now it's just a matter of which one is sharp in practice."
DANIELE SAUVAGEAU

February 13	Women
SWEDEN 7 KAZAKHSTAN 0	
2 p.m.	**The Peaks**

Sweden had an easy time in its 7-0 victory over the Kazakh women. By an interesting coincidence, this was the same score by which the Kazakhs lost to Canada the day before. Captain Erika Holst had two goals and two assists and Maria Roth added a goal and two helpers to pace Sweden, which outshot Kazahstan 43-17. The game was a chippy affair as the teams combined for 23 minor penalties and 46 penalty minutes. After the win, Sweden would have two days to tune up for its toughest game of the preliminary round, a February 16 date with the powerful Canadian team.

Pat Quinn and Mario Lemieux Meet the Press

"My aim is to win in regulation time. Sixty minutes. Sunday afternoon. I've already seen it." — Pat Quinn, February 13, 2002

"I haven't been playing back-to-back games to make sure that I could get to the Olympics. I'm looking forward to the chance to play with these great players and bringing a gold medal back to Canada." — Mario Lemieux, February 13, 2002

For the second time today, members of Canada's vaunted men's Olympic team met with reporters to discuss the team and the upcoming games which begin Friday afternoon at the E-Center against Sweden. Tonight it was coach Pat Quinn and captain Mario Lemieux behind the microphones at the Main Press Centre in downtown Salt Lake City.

They addressed all the pertinent issues surrounding the tournament and the first game. "I think we'll pretty much play a 1-2-2 formation because most of the teams are playing that or a variation with some subtle change to it," Quinn revealed. On the matter of developing a cohesive unit within 24 hours of the team's first game, Quinn addressed the format of the medals round as being to his advantage. "We have five days and three games to shortcut the team-building concept," he said of his intention to use this time to create a team from scratch. "We don't have to win any of the games to advance, though we intend to win all three."

On his team's style of play and his chalkboard philosophy with x's and o's, Quinn said he wanted to keep things simple: "We don't have much practise time, so we're trying to get some balance. But we want to change the way of thinking for a Canadian team. We've found overseas that dumping the puck in won't work, so we're not going to just give

> "Obviously, we have to take some shortcuts in team building. But there are some pretty great players coming here. We have five days and three games to shortcut the team-building concept. Those three games we don't have to win, but we intend to win them. Then we have three games we have to win. The progress in those first three games is huge."
> **PAT QUINN**

them the puck here," he noted indirectly of his desire to ice a skating team built on speed and offense.

Quinn, like Curtis Joseph earlier in the day, sees no emotional problem with finding ways to check his NHL team's top scorer, Mats Sundin of Toronto, when Canada faces Sweden on Friday. "We've all grown up as competitors and we live in an era where people change teams a lot more than they used to, so I don't see it [teammates becoming opponents overnight] as being a problem."

He elaborated in the specific. "Mats is having the best year, if not of his career then in the time I've been around him. And like all great players, he has his tendencies. That's what makes him great. We'll have to identify those tendencies and try to work on those. We'll be ready," he said, nodding.

Judging by Quinn's indirect comments on who will play with whom, he'll likely pair teammates as much as possible, certainly in the early going. "It'll be different because usually you develop a team in stages. We don't have that time. Some players have been together, others you can see would like to be together. We have pairs of defencemen and pairs of forwards who have played a bit." One thing was almost certain, though — Paul Kariya would be on Mario Lemieux's left wing after their terrific performance at the recent All-Star Game in Los Angeles.

"We have a great team and a great chance to win a gold medal," Lemieux reiterated. I'm looking forward to getting going."

February 13   **Men**
SWITZERLAND 2 BELARUS 1
4 p.m.   **E-Center**

Switzerland salvaged a little pride from its disappointing play in the preliminary round with a 2-1 win over Belarus (Qualifier I). Jean-Jacques Aeschlimann of Lugano scored the winner midway through the second period. The other Swiss goal came from Patrick Fischer.

Vadim Bekbulatov replied for the Belarussians. Frustration boiled over between Swiss defenceman Olivier Keller and the slow-footed Oleg Antonenko early in the third as they scuffled to the tune of ten minutes in total penalties (four to Keller, six to Antonenko). Switzerland outshot Belarus 37-24. The news off the ice for Switzerland remained bad, however, as forwards Marcel Jenni and Reto von Arx were

sent home for spending a night carousing in downtown Salt Lake City. Even on the day they had to leave the Olympic Village, they took off for Los Angeles at 3 a.m. without notifying the Swiss hockey authorities, who had scheduled their departure to Europe for 7:15 that morning. Jenni and von Arx claimed that they were scapegoats for Switzerland's inability to advance to the final round.

February 13   **Men**
UKRAINE 4   **FRANCE 2**
7 p.m.   **The Peaks**

France suffered its second straight loss by a two-goal margin and its record fell to 1-2 as Ukraine triumphed 4-2. The win didn't do the

Ukrainians any good, as their opening 1-0 loss to Belarus meant that they had lost their opportunity of securing first place in Group B and moving into the final round, despite a solid 5-2 win over Switzerland. Veteran NHLer Dmitri Khristich scored a goal for Ukraine, as did Igor Chibirev,

Vadim Shakhraychuk, and Toronto prospect Alexei Ponikarovsky. French superstar Philippe Bozon scored both goals for his side. France tried unsuccessfully to get an extra goal by pulling netminder Cristobal Huet with 35 seconds remaining. Ukraine outshot France 32-31. 🍁

DAY 6

February 14   **Women**
FINLAND 3   **GERMANY 1**
11 a.m.   **The Peaks**

German goalie Stephanie Wartosch-Kurten had an excellent outing and Julia Wierscher managed to spoil

Tuula Puputti's shutout with six minutes to go, as Finland defeated Germany 3-1 in women's hockey. While Finland outshot the Germans 39-16 overall, the margin in the third period was much tighter (12-9). Wierscher's goal was the first by the German women at the Olympics. Finland improved its record here at Salt Lake to 2-0, getting goals from Katja Riipi, Oona Parviainen, and Hanne Sikio. This was the worst-attended of all the women's preliminary round games, yet still attracted an impressive 4,769 spectators.

February 14   **Men**
SWITZERLAND 4 AUSTRIA 1
3 p.m.   **E-Center**

After a poor start to Salt Lake with a 3-3 tie to France and a 5-2 loss to the Ukraine, Switzerland rallied to salvage some pride by winning its last game of the round robin 2-1 over Belarus and then defeated Austria in a classification game today by a 4-1 score.

The Swiss started on their heels in the first, taking four minor penalties and being outshot by Austria 22-9. Some fine goaltending, though, by Reinhard Divis kept the team in the game (coach Krueger elected to play Divis over NHLer David Aebischer, figuring the experience was greater for the youngster and the score of lesser importance).

Switzerland came to life in the second by scoring two goals, one by J.J. Aeschlimann and the other by Martin Pluss. Canadian-born Tommy Searle brought Austria to within one early in the third, but a goal by Julien Vauclair a short time later decided the game. Pluss scored again, into an empty net, at 19:20.

February 14   **Men**
LATVIA 9   **UKRAINE 2**
8 p.m.   **E-Center**

No team will win many hockey games after falling behind 6-0 in the first period. The Ukraines learned that rather obvious lesson the hard way against Latvia, showing a lack of discipline as they allowed two power play goals by the 5:56 mark of the opening period. Ukraine would go on to total 26 minutes in the sin bin, compared to Latvia's six. It was a night for the Latvians to bulk up their statistics. Igors Bondarevs led the way with a goal and two assists, and Vyacheslavs Fanduls scored twice. Sergejs Maticins had a goal and two assists, and Harijs Vitolins and Aleksandrs

Nizivijs had a goal and an assist, while Aleksandrs Kercs and Aleksandrs Macijevskis posted two assists apiece. Leonids Tambijevs, Gregorijs Pantelejevs, and Aleksandrs Semjonovs had one goal each. Ukraine's top netminder, Igor Karpenko, was replaced early in the first period in favour of Kostyantyn Simchuk.

When Dmitri Khristich finally scored for Ukraine midway through the second, the E-Center erupted (rather facetiously) with cheering as if someone had just won a gold medal. However, Igor Chibirev's goal less than four minutes later did not spark a miraculous Ukrainian comeback. The result gave Latvia ninth place in the tournament, while the Ukraine settled for tenth. ❖

February 14   **Women**
USA 12   **CHINA 1**
4 p.m.   **The Peaks**

A significant breach of slaughter di-plomacy occurred Thursday after-noon in the USA-China women's hockey game at the Peaks when Xiuqing Yang flipped the puck on goal just inside the centre line (see photos). The puck eked between the pads of goalie Sarah Tueting, and China narrowed the gap to 7-1. However, it was all U.S. before and after that as the red, white, and blue won 12-1, out-shooting the Chinese 71-10.

At the other end, Hong Guo was the story of the day, facing a deluge of rubber that did not abate for sixty minutes. Guo is one of only about a hundred women who play hockey in China and spends most of her time practising with the Chinese men's national team. "My only ex-posure to pro hockey was when I lived in Canada for eight months and was able to watch the NHL," she related with folklorish charm.

Guo loved the experience of fac-ing the Americans, though she truly felt she could have made more saves. "It's good practise for me to play a team with so much individual talent," she noted. The American lead was 3-0 after one period, but then they exploded for four goals in a span of 2:43 midway through the

second. Cammi Granato had three goals and Laurie Baker two.

The team lost Tricia Dunn after the first when she received a major and game misconduct for a hit from

behind as the first period ended. But on the ensuing power play to start the second, the United States outshot the Chinese 2-0 and then went on the attack.

American goalie Sarah Teuting misses a long shot from China's Xiuqing Yang and the puck slowly, agoniz-ingly slips between her pads and into the net for China's only goal of the game.

February 14   **Men**
SLOVAKIA 7   **FRANCE 1**
9 p.m.   **The Peaks**

Slovakia sleepwalked through this late-starting placement match and put France to bed with a four-goal outburst in the third period that sealed a solid 7-1 win. Rastislav

Pavlikovsky had three points and Marian Hossa three goals and an assist in the final game of Slovakia's tournament, while Dusan Milo got a pair of assists. The top French scorer, Maurice Rozenthal, spoiled the shutout bid of Slovak netminder Rastislav Stana with less than a minute to go in the third. Slovakia

achieved a 49-19 advantage in shots on goal. Getting thirteenth place in-stead of fourteenth was little conso-lation to the Slovaks, who before com-ing to Salt Lake City had been touted as potential medal prospects. General manager Peter Stastny was nonethe-less pleased with his player's efforts under the circumstances.

DAY 7

SWEDEN 5
CANADA 2

February 15   **Men**
4:10 p.m.   **E-Center**

'Big ice hockey' defeated good old Canadian hockey as Sweden beat Canada 5-2. "We got beat soundly," coach Pat Quinn acknowledged afterward.

While Mats Sundin played an important role in Tre Kronor's win, in at least small measure because of his knowledge of Canadian goalie Curtis Joseph, Quinn elected not to dress Ryan Smyth, the only Edmonton Oilers forward on the team and the one who knew Swedish goalie Tommy Salo the best. "We elected to go with experience today," Quinn explained. "Ryan will play Saturday. Would he have been a factor today? I don't know. Hindsight is terrific."

Swedish coach Hardy Nilsson kept his game plan simple — and effective. "We don't call it Torpedo hockey as you in the media call it," he explained. "We call it 'big ice hockey,' to create more ice and space and keep the puck. We know as long as we have the puck, it's easier to play them."

The energy and tension in the E-Center this afternoon for the game was palpable an hour before the 4:10 p.m. start.

GAME SUMMARY

First Period

1	Canada, Blake (Peca, Fleury)	2:37
2	Sweden, Sundin (Alfredsson)	5:30
	penalties: Sundin (Swe)	11:31

Second Period

3	Sweden, Sundstrom (Nylander, Naslund)	6:06
4	Sweden, Sundin (Alfredsson, Lidstrom)	10:42
5	Sweden, Jonsson (Zetterberg)	11:47
6	Sweden, Dahlen (Sundstrom, Sundin)	15:58
	penalties: MacInnis (Can)	15:18

Third Period

7	Canada, Brewer (Nolan)	15:39
	penalties: Olausson (Swe)	0:27
	Ragnarsson (Swe)	7:16

In Goal

CANADA	Curtis Joseph
SWEDEN	Tommy Salo

Shots on Goal

CANADA	15	3	17	35
SWEDEN	10	11	4	25

Referee	Dennis LaRue
Linesmen	Dan Schachte/Sergei Kulakov

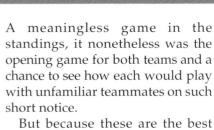

A meaningless game in the standings, it nonetheless was the opening game for both teams and a chance to see how each would play with unfamiliar teammates on such short notice.

But because these are the best players in the world, they put on a show of speed, strength, and skill that Salt Lake was seeing for the first time (Belarus could not inspire such a performance from Russia, but the

Russians would be heard from in due course).

Canada scored first and early on a nice pass up the middle from Michael Peca to Rob Blake who had about three seconds to wind up and fire. He drove a terrific shot that flew between the legs of Tommy Salo.

And then it happened. The first showdown of these Games. Mats Sundin took a perfect long pass from Daniel Alfredsson and went in alone on Maple Leafs teammate Curtis

Joseph — and Sundin won round one with a slight fake and perfect shot between Joseph's legs. "Once the game starts, you're playing the other team," Sundin said. "That's

hockey. Who knows? If we meet later on in the tournament he might not let anything in."

The rest of the period was high tempo, end-to-end action. The edge went to Canada with some excellent scoring chances (including a post) and some great defense from their huge and mobile blueline corps. The Swedes generated some possession of their own, often with the long pass they love to employ, but their defence did show signs of vulnerability.

In the second, all hell broke loose. Sweden found its legs and style of play, and Canada fell apart. Niklas Sundstrom scored when he took a pass from the corner and outwaited Joseph to lift the puck over him. Mats Sundin scored another goal when he wired a slapshot that deflected off Rob Blake's stick, and he added an assist on Ulf Dahlen's goal. But the story was how effective Tre Kronor was at using the full ice. All four of their second-period goals were the result of long passes that caught Canada by surprise, most notably Kenny Jonsson who broke in alone and scored stickside. Sweden outshot Canada 11-3 in that period.

"We started off hesitant, but in the second period, there were about ten minutes that was the best part of the game for us," Mattias Norstrom said.

In the third, Canada again reasserted itself, creating numerous chances but being thwarted by Salo. Fleury, Lemieux, Gagne, and Lindros

all had great scoring opportunities before Eric Brewer, of all people, scored on a partial breakaway. Canada scored again moments later, but referee Denis LaRue ruled that Michael Peca was in the crease, thus denying Lindros a goal and the Canadians a potential late comeback.

Like the rest of the team, Curtis Joseph put in a performance beset by bad luck and timing. Five goals in two periods certainly indicated that Martin Brodeur deserved the next start, but Quinn squashed that hypothesis immediately. "We've had a plan for the goaltenders coming in, and I'm not going to break down a trust we're trying to build. In the end, it really doesn't matter whether we won or lost tonight."

In truth, though, goaltending was the difference in the game. Joseph did not play at his best, and Salo did. "Tommy made some big saves for us. He kept us in the game early on," Sundin said.

Joseph was hardly the only problem, though. Mario Lemieux looked lost on the right wing, and Eric Lindros looked slow on the bigger ice surface. Captain Lemieux remained unfazed. "That's the beauty of the Olympics. We have two more games to go before the tournament starts," he said by way of admitting that victory against qualifier Germany was not requisite.

Notes: Pat Quinn's lines were as follows: Sakic, Kariya, Lemieux; Yzerman, Shanahan, Iginla; Lindros, Nolan, Gagne; Peca, Fleury, Nieuwendyk. For Sweden, coach Hardy Nilsson used these combinations: Sundin, Dahlen, Alfredsson; Naslund, Sundstrom, Nylander; Axelsson, Arvedson, Johansson; Renberg, Zetterberg, Jonsson... One humourous moment occurred during the few minutes prior to the start of the game when captains Lemieux and Sundin didn't know when to ex-

change gifts. Nor did they shake hands with the referee and linesmen prior to the opening faceoff, some-thing unfamiliar to both of them in the NHL but a long standing tradition in international play. ❦

"I was probably just like everyone else in Canada—we were all surprised. Anything that's worthwhile getting is hard to get. We knew that coming in this was not going to be a cakewalk, and maybe the fact that our players saw and realized that in game one, that it isn't going to be a cakewalk, that they're in for a dogfight, and that the Swedes are a great team, and Mats Sundin is a great player, Salo is a great goaltender... they played as a team and they deserved to beat us. We have to have that same theory with our team. We need our guys to play great, but we have to play better as a team, and that's what's going to carry us."
PAUL KARIYA

February 15   Men
RUSSIA 6   BELARUS 4
11 a.m.   E-Center

The Russians may have defeated Belarus 6-4 this afternoon, but it wasn't the one-sided, lopsided game everyone was expecting. Sergei Samsonov scored at 1:45 on an easy-looking pass from Ilya Kovalchuk, and the rest of the period looked almost as easy.

The game was a mismatch in so many ways, yet such is hockey that superior skill does not always triumph on the scoreboard. In pure skill terms, this was Manhattan playing the Bronx, the cool, slick Russians simply looking better than Belarus. Their equipment looked better, their sticks newer and shinier, even their smiles more polished. When Russia iced the puck, they flicked it hard in the air 200 feet and the puck didn't wobble a centimetre until it hit the glass at the far end. Their passes were quicker, harder, more accurate, and they skated circles around the Belarussians on many occasions.

When the Russians carried the puck, they never looked down; heads up, they skated looking for the available man and not down to double-check to see that the puck was still there. When they scored, they made it look easy and only Alexei Yashin celebrated like he had just won the Stanley Cup.

The Russians often looked like they were playing in an All-Star Game. One hand on the stick, they'd circle in their own zone and try to go end-to-end, only to be stopped. They made play look easy not just because of technical superiority (which it was) but because they made an effort to do so. They were much better than

their opponents, they knew it, and they wanted to show it.

Yet the score wasn't 10-0. It was 6-4. Nikolai Khabibulin had an off game in net, but as Igor Larionov said to the delight of a packed press corps when asked about having such a great goalie on the team, "we don't have any choices," a reference to goaltending being the country's weakest area. Although the Russians have many outstanding young players—Kovalchuk and Maxim Afinogenov, for example—their number-two goalie here was Yegor Podomatsky.

The Belarussians made the game exciting in the second when they outshot Russia 18-8 and outscored the mighty team 2-1, but two phenomenal shots early in the third sealed the game for Russia. Nonetheless, Russia must become a team and a not a group of individuals. The players must learn each other's moves and not rely on the player to overcome or replace the team. But at least they have an excellent starting point

February 15   Women
RUSSIA 4   KAZAKHSTAN 1
2 p.m.   The Peaks

The biggest former Soviet republic dominated its little cousin in the only women's hockey game of the day as Russia cruised to a 4-1 victory. Final shots ran 52-18 in Russia's favour, and it was a credit to Kazakh goalie Natalya Trunova that the score was tied 1-1 after the first period. With the Russians in full control in the final 20 minutes, the pace lulled visibly as the teams combined for seven minor penalties. Ekaterina Pachkevitch, Svetlana Terentieva, Tatiana Burina, and Tatiana Tsareva scored the goals for Russia, while Natalya Yakovchuk had the lone score for Kazakhstan. Russia's Ekaterina Smolentseva added a pair of assists.

— a fast, young, highly-skilled team that's also a pleasure to watch.

February 15 Men
CZECH 8
GERMANY 2
7 p.m. The Peaks

Hockey players are not known for their braggadocio. Even the Czechs, the so-called "Italians of European hockey," were avoiding predictions about this Olympic tournament.

They got off on the

right foot Friday, pounding Germany 8-2. They showed an ability to break down Hans Zach's defensive system, which so frustrated Slovakia in the preliminary round.

The win also had "revenge" written all over it. The Germans spoiled Czech hopes in the 1996 World Cup by applying a 7-1 drubbing.

"It was in the back of our minds," admitted Pittsburgh centre Robert Lang, a member of that 1996 team. "Whenever you play against the Germans, you never know what you're going to get. They usually play pretty tight hockey and good defense."

Well, Friday they sure didn't. But the Czechs knew they hadn't won anything yet.

"It was a pretty high-scoring game yesterday and I don't think it's going to stay like that," Czech captain Jaromir Jagr said. "Defense is going to win it, for sure."

Jagr's four-point effort against Germany created some early hope that the Czechs will be able to mount an effective attack against Sweden's "big ice hockey," which largely shut down Canada's offense in a 5-2 win.

Watch for their continued reliance on a 2-3 forechecking system that both clogs the neutral zone and provides counterattack opportunities. It was the key to their 1998 Olympic victory and three consecutive IIHF World Championships since then.

Of course, you can't overlook Dominik Hasek between the pipes. But the Czechs seem weary of the

popular myth cultivated in North America, which alleges that Hasek won the gold in Nagano all by himself.

"Everybody's going to rely on their goaltenders in this tournament, so I don't see any reason why we wouldn't rely on him," said Robert Lang. "He was a huge part of '98 and he's going to be a big part of this team. Whoever has a hot goaltender is going to do well."

Mario Lemieux's goalie, Curtis Joseph, was ice-cold in allowing five goals against the Swedes. But the Czechs, many of whom have played with Lemieux, respect his team. They can't understand the media controversy in Pittsburgh about Super Mario's remark that his current focus is the Olympics.

"There is nothing you can really do," said Lang. "You just have to play and do your job. If he decides to take some time off and play the Olympics, hey, it's his decision. He's the captain and the owner. It's up to him and [GM] Craig [Patrick]. That's how it is."

"I'm worrying about my team and about Washington," Jagr said. "I'm here in Salt Lake City. I don't know what [the Pittsburgh fans] think."

"We'll let the media do their work," added Lang. "We just want to play hockey." ♦

February 15 Men – USA 6 Finland 0 – 8:45 p.m. E-Center

This game was just what American fans wanted to see. The United States won the battles along the boards and kept the play wide open. John LeClair kickstarted the USA's tournament with a hat trick, banging in rebounds and finishing off a two-on-one with Brett Hull. Third-time Olympian Mike Dunham recorded the shutout, getting the surprise start in goal over Mike Richter. Finland's top line of Sami Kapanen with Jere Lehtinen and Teemu Selanne registered only eight shots on goal. Finnish goalie Jani Hurme started off confidently but was over-challenging wildly by the end of the game. "In Nagano, we had trouble scoring some goals, so to be able to put six on the board and win is excellent," said LeClair. "We've got to play way smarter than this," said Selanne, who was irked by the USA's superior use of the big ice surface. "But I still have a good feeling about this. It's only one game." Afterwards, all the talk was about the USA's anticipated confrontation with the Russians the following day.

DAY
8

CANADA 11
SWEDEN 0

**February 16   Women
7:00 p.m.   The Peaks**

Playing its first game of the tournament at The Peaks, Canada got its offense in gear with an 11-0 thrashing of Sweden, outshooting the opposition 70-22. After a slow start

(1-0 after the first period), Canada exploded for four goals in the second and six in the third. Jennifer Botterill had two goals and an assist and Jayna Hefford added a goal and three assists to lead the charge.

"It was nice to see the floodgates open," said Hayley Wickenheiser of the offensive outburst. "We're gelling at the right time," added Tammy Lee Shewchuk. "We're getting in front of the net, getting our sticks down to get those all-important rebounds." The game also provided goalie Kim St. Pierre with her second shutout of the tournament. Her Swedish counterpart, Annika Ahlen, managed 18 saves in the first period before

(top) The Canadian women celebrate one of eleven goals they scored on Sweden in preliminary round action while (right) Cassie Campbell establishes herself in front of Tre Kronor goalie Annika Ahlen.

First Period

1 Canada, Botterill		
(Shewchuk, Bechard)		10:26
penalties: Dupuis (Can)		7:19

Second Period

2 Canada, Piper (unassisted)		6:01
3 Canada, Botterill		
(Heaney, Hefford)		9:12
4 Canada, Wickenheiser		
(Campbell, Goyette)		12:06
5 Canada, Campbell (Goyette)		17:18
penalties: Roth (Swe)		2:27
Roth (Swe)		7:18
Jansson (Swe)		12:41

Third Period

6 Canada, Ouellette (unassisted)		2:42
7 Canada, Hefford (Dupuis)		3:05
8 Canada, Dupuis (unassisted)		6:52
9 Canada, Sunohara (Hefford)		15:21
10 Canada, Antal		
(Botterill, Brisson)		19:37
11 Canada, Chartrand		
(Hefford, Ouellette)		19:54
penalties: Brisson (Can)		13:26
(Swe-too many men)		14:48
Ahlen (Swe)		16:26
Andersson (Swe)		17:37
Roth (Swe)		18:47

In Goal

CANADA	Kim St. Pierre
SWEDEN	Annika Ahlen

Shots on Goal

CANADA	19	18	33	70
SWEDEN	6	10	6	22

Referee	Anu Hirvonen
Linesmen	Marina Konstantinova
	Tina Kirschner

the onslaught proved too much for her to handle.

Despite the perception of the women's tournament as a two-horse race between Canada and the USA, the Canadians didn't want to get overly confident heading into their semi-finals matchup against Finland on Tuesday. "Finland is a team to be reckoned with," said Cassie Campbell. "Yes, the USA beat them handily, but they've only lost to the USA and ourselves at the world championships by one goal. They are a great offensive team." But on the whole, Canada had to be optimistic heading into the playoffs. "We finished with an 11-0 game against Sweden, which was our best competition in the pool," said St. Pierre. "So I think we're just getting better and better."

"We had a good game, obviously. This is exactly where we wanted to be and now we have a couple of days to get ready for the semi-finals."
DANIELE SAUVAGEAU

"We wanted to focus on finishing each play that we made. It was great because so many people contributed today. I think it was just a solid team effort. With everyone around you doing so well, it was easy to do a good job."

"I think our team is really starting to come together. Everyone just felt the energy. The crowd was great today. I just think a confident attitude came with it."
JENNIFER BOTTERILL

Canada's Colleen Sostorics tries to make her way by a Swedish opponent during the 11-0 win for the Canadians.

Martin Brodeur will start in goal. Michael Peca is relieved to be back at centre. Joe Sakic is no longer playing with Mario Lemieux. Lemieux might be suffering from a hip injury that will force him to miss action in the next day or two. Pat Quinn promised no changes yesterday, but after meetings with Wayne Gretzky has changed his mind. All in an off-day's work. And while there is talk of Lemieux taking one of the next two games off, Gretzky said Mario practised today and is ready to go for tomorrow.

"It's an exciting time," said Brodeur, benefactor of Quinn's change of plans to the goaltending rotation. "I'm going to stay a little deeper in my net and not challenge as much," he revealed of his international strategy. Despite his extraordinary success in the NHL, Brodeur's national team dossier is almost completely empty. He was backup in 1998 in Nagano and didn't play particularly well in either the 1996 World Cup or the '97 World Championships, and he has yet to win a game in a Team Canada sweater. He is making history, however. As soon as he plays one minute tomorrow night against Germany, he and his father, Denis, will be the first father-son team in the Olympics for Canada. Denis played goal in 1956 in Cortina.

"Defensively, you have to be aware of the long pass and offensively you have to be able to take advantage of it," Michael Peca said.

"Basically, though, we have to come back and have a guy available for our defencemen and support from there with speed. We could try to change our game and try to learn, but there's no way we have the time to learn. We've got to keep it simple and play the game we know how to play."

"They changed up the lines today," Sakic revealed when asked about sticking with Lemieux and Sakic. "We still have two more games to find out the line combinations and what works for us."

As for Peca, he is as relieved as anyone on the team. "For me, it was a little tough to start out on the wing. It's a different system and a totally different game, but I know they want me to be the guy down low in our end most of the time, so it's better that I play in the middle than on the wing."

"What we learned is that offensively we can just play the way we know how to play and be successful with it," Peca observed. "We shouldn't be worrying about playing our own form of torpedo offense. For a while there yesterday our forwards were freelancing, trying to come up with our own breakouts and breakaway plans. We weren't really doing what we set out to accomplish. We were standing around too much and not generating enough speed."

"We need to shorten our game up," coach Quinn surmised after yesterday's "stinker" as Gretzky

dubbed the 5-2 loss. "We still have to create some room, but we can't have three guys turn their back on the play and fly up ice hoping to get the puck. That's not the way Canadian players play."

"It's not so much what we've learned today so much as what we didn't do," Jarome Iginla said. "We tried to stretch the ice and got pretty spread out and we weren't supporting each other and giving each other good outs and coming up with speed. We looked at the tapes today and talked about it, and it was really ten minutes that got away from us when we stood around watching Sweden work their stuff."

Defenceman Rob Blake agreed. "We should do what we do in North America. We play as a group of five. We're not used to having guys running out to the far blueline for that long pass. We never played that way; we're not going to play that way now."

Like many on the team, he watched much of the USA-Finland game that followed. "The Americans supported the puck very well to create turnovers, and when you do that you can use the no-red line to your advantage. The good thing the U.S. did was create a ton of turnovers."

"We're still a confident team and feel we can win the gold medal," Peca said.

"We know if we just go out and play our own game and settle down, we'll be fine," Lindros added, with confidence.

February 16 **Women**
USA 5 **FINLAND 0**
11 a.m. **E-Center**

The hockey world doesn't yet have to learn how to ask 'do you believe in miracles?' in Finnish, but it's clear the Suomis are the best women's team in the world after Canada and the USA. Despite losing 5-0 to the USA, they showed much skill with the puck and ability to check and skate a bit with the Americans.

The shot clock, in fact, read in the Finns' favour for a brief time midway through the game when they recorded their fifth shot to USA's three at 9:17. The Americans, though, scored a short time later after killing off a five-on-three shorthanded situation and dominated the rest of the period.

Eighteen-year-old Natalie Darwitz led the Americans with her first Olympic hat trick and now leads the team with seven points in three games. "Although she's young in years," coach Ben Smith noted, "she's not young in experience. She's been to three World Championships and now an Olympics."

If nothing else, the game marked the third in a row in which the Americans started the first period off slowly, a potentially bad habit when they meet Canada in the finals. "I think it takes a lot of teams a shift or two just to get your legs going," A.J. Mleczko said, unworried. "But overall, I'm not concerned about that at all."

The game featured fine goaltending at both ends. For the Finns, Tuula Puputti faced 47 shots and

stopped three breakaways in the second period alone. And, for the first time, Sara DeCosta had to make several fine stops of her own against a Finish team that showed an ability to create a forecheck and force turnovers. They had a number of good scoring chances, particularly in the second when the United States scored the only goal of the period.

"Yeah," Mleczko agreed, "for the first time she faced some really tough shots. But we've done a great job in practise with her, just firing a lot of pucks at our goaltenders.

any defensive lapses by the Americans "They have a lot of speed. They have some stickhandlers, but I'm really happy with the way we played defensively tonight," Mleczko added.

The game wasn't dirty by any means, but referee Jacqui Palm did call 24 minor penalties, including a minor and misconduct to Petra Vaarakallio for hitting from behind.

"We're getting there," was Mleczko's assessment of the team's progress. "This team isn't going to get faster or quicker or sharper.

They're tough to beat." No more evident were DeCosta's contributions than in that five-on-three in the first when she made three fine saves before the Americans came down the ice to open the scoring.

Finland's chances were the result of skill and hard work more than

We're just here to play and have fun while we're doing it."

That concludes the round robin for both teams, and playoff matches will be determined tonight after Germany plays China and Canada faces Sweden at The Peaks. ♁

February 16   Women
GERMANY 5   CHINA 5
2 p.m.   The Peaks

Michaela Lanzl capped a remarkable third period comeback by the Germans with a goal at 18:19 to give her team a 5-5 tie with the Chinese. China had overcome an early goal to the Germans to take a 5-2 lead after 40 minutes and seemed certain of victory when the final period began. Nina Ritter scored just 1:37 into the game, but Rui Sun came back four minutes later to tie the score. The Chinese broke the game open in the second period with four goals, including two from Hongmei Liu, to just one from the Germans. In the third, China seemed in control until the German attack became effective midway through and resulted in three unanswered goals. The tie confirmed China's playoff round matchup with Russia, while the Germans would face Kazakhstan on Sunday.

February 16   Men
FINLAND 8   BELARUS 1
4:45 p.m.   E-Center

Firing only 21 shots (four and six in the first two periods, respectively) cost Belarus its second game of the final round at the E-Center as Finland roared to an 8-1 victory.

Teemu Selanne and Olli Jokinen sparked the Finnish attack with two goals apiece. Sami Kapanen, Tomi Kallio, Aki-Petteri Berg, and Mikko Eloranta added singles for the victorious Finns.

Vasily Pankov had the lone goal for the Belarussians, who have now surrendered 14 goals in two final round matchups. Atlanta prospect Pasi Nurminen started in goal for Finland in place of Jani Hurme, who had allowed six goals against the United States.

The Finns were playing their second game in 20 hours, but came out with good jump and defensive poise and visibly disheartened by Friday's 6-0 loss to the USA.

Finland opened the scoring at 1:30 on a fluke goal by Jokinen, who centred the puck from the right corner and banked it off a Belarus defender through the legs of goalie Sergei Shabanov.

Selanne scored on a rebound at the side of the net during a Finnish power play at 14:53. Shabanov was yanked in favor of Mezin right after the Finns took the 2-0 lead. Jokinen made it 3-0 for the Finns with his second goal at 16:24 when he accepted a pass from Tomi Kallio in the slot and one-timed it past Mezin.

Selanne then scored Finland's fourth goal at 4:55 of the second after his team worked the puck around the Belarus zone brilliantly as if they were on a power play.

Belarus finally spoiled Nurminen's shutout bid at 3:54 of the final period on a power play when Vasily Pankov tipped in a Ruslan Salei point shot.

The Leafs' Finn, Aki-Petteri Berg scored with a blast from the line that dribbled through Mezin's pads at 9:21 of the third. Raimo Helminen got an assist on the goal. The veteran now has points in each of the record six Olympic hockey tournaments in which he has played. Mikko Eloranta added one more to seal the deal for Finland with about five minutes remaining. ❦

February 16　　　　**Men**
RUSSIA 2　　　　**USA 2**
9:30 p.m.　　　　**E-Center**

A classic. One for the ages. A barnburner. End to end. No holds barred. What hockey is all about. A pace so fast it'll be hard to go back to a slower game. The opening faceoff took place at 9:31 p.m., and the game ended in a 2-2 tie at 11:39 p.m. Said an exhausted Brian Rolston, "It was so fast out there you just didn't have much time; you just had to keep your feet moving as much as possible."

The U.S. has defeated Russia exactly twice in Olympic competition—3-2 in 1960 at Squaw Valley and 4-3 in 1980 in Lake Placid. Both were gold medal Olympics for America, and both, not surprisingly, came on American soil.

The E-Center in 2002 was not without its residue of that Miracle on Ice, either. Behind the Russian bench were Vladislav Tretiak, starting goalie in 1980, and his all-star superstar defenceman, Slava Fetisov, and behind the United States bench was none other than Herb Brooks, the man who guided that miracle team to gold.

Perhaps the bigger story was not the score but instead a more symbolic element. Here we were, on U.S. land again, for the most anticipated game of the Olympics for the hometown fans. It's a Saturday night, and game time goes at 11:30 p.m. Eastern Standard Time. Hockey is still not given its due by United States networks, though Brooks declined to offer an opinion of his own. "You'd have to talk to the TV station about the start time, but it certainly was atypical and throws the players off – but both teams have to deal with it."

To start the first, both teams came out with speed, finesse, strength, and emotion—and it only got better as time passed. The transition game was lightning quick, and although the Russians didn't get their first shot until almost nine minutes in, the teams had an equal number of excellent chances and both Mike Richter and Nikolai Khabibulin made some fine saves to ensure a goalless first.

Richter then stole the show in the second as Russia outshot the home side 17-4. The USA converted a five-on-three when Khabibulin failed to hold the puck and Keith Tkachuk jammed it home. But the Russians were relentless. Richter stoned Ilya Kovalchuk on a breakaway, made pad saves, glove saves, post-to-post saves. He looked like vintage '96 Richter in the blue ice.

Finally, on a power play, Valeri Bure converted a cross-ice pass, delaying the one-timer until Richter had stacked the pads and then finding the gap as the goalie tried to kick his top pad high.

The third was more of the same, except faster and more intense over the last five minutes. Russia scored early in the period when Sergei Fedorov banged in a rebound, and then they played puck possession for about half the period. But slowly, patiently, surely the Americans created a few chances. With just 4:30 to go, Brett Hull knocked in his own rebound and the game went into the books as a thrilling tie.

If hockey fans could see hockey like this every night, they'd never, ever want to leave the building. ❧

DAY 9

CANADA 3 GERMANY 2

**February 17   Men
7:00 p.m. The Peaks**

Not only did Canada beat Germany by the slimmest of scores, 3-2, but to add insult to injury the Germans didn't even pull their goalie in the final minute when they had possession in the Canadian end. "A point against Canada would not have helped us in the standings," coach Hans Zach explained, "and an empty net goal would have been bad for our self-confidence."

Mario Lemieux was in the building, but he wasn't on the ice. Pat Quinn revamped his lines and put Martin Brodeur in the net, but still Canada came out and played a tentative first period that ended in a scoreless tie. Germany, in fact, had the better of the play in the early going, and when Canada did pick up the attack, the players got nervous around the goal. Michael Peca fanned on a shorthanded breakaway, and there were other chances that were flubbed. "We seemed pretty tight early on," Quinn admitted. "Our guys were too ready if anything. That's what caused all the tension."

One could hear the collective sigh of relief in the second when Joe Sakic converted a lovely Simon Gagne pass in front to open the scoring midway through the second. The

GAME SUMMARY

First Period

No scoring

penalties: Lindros (Can)	0:24
Ehrhoff (Ger)	7:59
Pronger (Can)	13:00

Second Period

1	Canada, Sakic (Gagne)	8:59
2	Canada, Kariya (Nolan)	14:23
3	Canada, Foote (Jovanovski, Nieuwendyk)	18:25
	penalties: Blake (Can)	4:35
	Kunce (Ger-major, misconduct)	13:24

Third Period

4	Germany, Loth (MacKay, Ludemann)	7:36
5	Germany, Hecht (Schubert, Abstreiter)	13:51
	penalties: Lindros (Can)	3:19
	MacInnis (Can)	12:16

In Goal

CANADA	Martin Brodeur
GERMANY	Marc Seliger

Shots on Goal

CANADA	10	17	10	37
GERMANY	8	4	8	20

Referee	Bill McCreary
Linesmen	Tim Nowak/Johan Norrman

"It's a win. Obviously we had a lot of chances and we didn't bear down. Well, we bore down, but we didn't seem to find the back of the net. I thought overall there was some progress made. That was different style of game than we are accustomed to seeing. They're a team that, when they sit back and play that one-four, they have a lot of energy left at the end of the game and they have to go for the offense. They basically played one period where they went for it and they got a couple of bounces and it went off the top of Marty's (Brodeur) stick and went in, but that's going to happen from time to time."
ERIC LINDROS

team got a huge break when NHL ref Bill McCreary called a major and game misconduct on Daniel Kunce for a hit to the head that drew blood, a play he originally called two minutes until consulting with European linesman Johan Norrman. Canada scored once on a power play and once more one second after another had expired.

The Germans broke Martin Brodeur's shutout when Andreas Loth scored in the third, and then another goal six minutes later created a more tense ending than Pat Quinn had hoped for. Canada's new lines weren't much more effective than the previous game, and the players didn't go to the net with any intensity or purpose. Although the team used the far blueline with greater effect than in game one, too often players would attempt the solo dash in favour of short, quick passes.

Afterward, players seemed overwhelmed by relief for victory but perfectly aware that their play tonight would result in a Czech slaughter on Monday night if they played no better. Martin Brodeur faced 20 shots and had some bad luck

"It was a good relief to get on board. We were generating a lot of chances, but it just wasn't going in. It was nice to get on the board and get the next two, especially after the first two periods where we skated well. We knew it was going to be tight with the one-four formation, but we hung in there and kept going."
JOE SAKIC

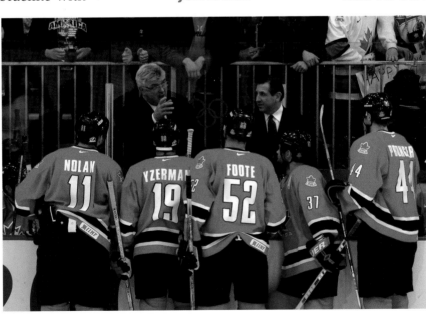

on the goals, and Quinn suggested the goalie lottery had yet to be held for the Czech game. "I may even use Belfour," he said to underline his exasperation with the netminding question.

Nonetheless, the concerns were there. Canada scored three goals on Seliger and two on Salo and the team had Dominik Hasek up next. Wherefore the offense? "Forty shots," Theo Fleury said. "No disrespect to them, but I don't think they contained us." Joe Sakic concurred: "We were generating chances but just weren't scoring. We knew it would be tight with their one-four, but a win's a win and we'll take it." Well, if coach Zach is able to come up with a plan to defend the best team in Canada, a coaching job in the NHL can't be far behind for the apparently brilliant bench boss.

The score didn't lie, though. So how should this result have been interpreted? Was progress being made or was the scoring team that Wayne Gretzky put together not as offensively talented as he had hoped? It took the team nearly seven min-

utes to get a single shot, and although the team had plenty of puck possession, they couldn't finish with the Olympian skill needed to go deep into the elimination round.

"We made some progress and we'll be better tomorrow," Quinn promised confidently.

Canada went with four lines tonight: Kariya, Lindros, Nolan; Gagne, Yzerman, Iginla; Sakic, Nieuwendyk, Smyth; Fleury, Peca, Shanahan. When he first got to Salt Lake, Quinn talked of keeping pairs of players together, but although Fleury and Lindros are two-thirds

"The other night against Sweden, we were way ahead of the play and had our back to the defenceman with the puck. You're not going to create a lot through the neutral zone. We did a lot better through the neutral zone. It took us a period to finally find it. They are lining up four across the blue line and they are having some success with it. It was big on the power play to capitalize on two."

MICHAEL PECA

of the highest-scoring line in the NHL, he has yet to play them side by side and find a Michael York-type Canadian as a third. "There's some tinkering with line combinations, but we don't have a lot of time," Sakic said. "But I don't think it's that difficult to get to know each other out there."

And Lemieux for Monday? "There's nothing definite on Mario now," was all Quinn would say, sounding like a man who wanted to save number 66 for the playoffs. Steve Yzerman acted as captain in place of the injured Lemieux. ❦

(top) *Canada's men celebrate a goal against Germany in the second period during a 3-2 win that was closer and more dramatic than coach Quinn would have liked.*

(previous) *Canada's Joe Nieuwendyk gets high-fives from teammates after his setup led to Adam Foote's goal that gave Canada a 3-0 lead in the second period. The goal turned out to be the game winner.*

February 17   **Women**
RUSSIA 4   **CHINA 1**
2 p.m.   **The Peaks**

The Bear and the Dragon put on a decent show for the fans. China looked good early in this one but couldn't sustain its momentum. The Russians fell behind quickly when Xiuqing Yang beat Irina Gashennikova to open the scoring at 1:12. But in the second period, Russia got three goals in a span of 2:42 from Larisa Mishina, Ekaterina Pachkevitch, and Tatiana Burina to take an insurmountable 3-1 lead. A goal from Tatiana Tsareva completed the win for Russia, which fired 41 shots at Chinese goaltender Hong Guo, who stands 5'11" and is nicknamed "The Great Wall of China."

February 17   **Women**
GERMANY 4 **KAZAKHSTAN 0**
9 p.m.   **E-Center**

Germany pulled off its 4-0 shutout victory despite being outshot 26-21 by the upstart Kazakhs. That margin was a welcome relief for Kazakh goalie Natalya Trunova, who had faced close to 200 shots in just four previous games in Salt Lake. Despite the loss, it was clear the Kazakhs were improving after suffering thrashings from Canada and Sweden. Germany's offensive leader was Maritta Becker with two goals. Singles came from Michaela Lanzl and Claudia Grundmann. Near the end of the game, play became decidedly chippy and the teams combined for 14 minutes in penalties in the third period.

February 17   **Men**
SWEDEN 2   **CZECH 1**
4 p.m.   **E-Center**

Mats Sundin scored early in the second period to lift Sweden to a 2-1 victory over the Czech Republic in final round action Sunday evening. Kim Johnsson had the other goal for Sweden, while Jiri Dopita replied for the Czechs.

Tommy Salo emerged as a hero for Tre Kronor for the second straight game, stopping 37 shots for the win.

Sweden demonstrated great composure in the first period, unconcerned about their opponent's status as defending Olympic and three-time world champions. They maintained their efficient puck movement, although the Czechs refused to get spread out as Canada had.

When the Czechs got into penalty trouble, derisive whistles from their fans filled the E-Center. Hasek was probably as upset with the constant presence of Detroit teammate Tomas Holmstrom's rear end in his face during the Swedish man advantage. Number 96's agitation played a role in the first Swedish goal, as

Johnsson blew a low point shot past Hasek with plenty of traffic in front at 4:45.

Sundin upped the score at 5:14 of the second, coming off the side boards and taking a short windup to slap the puck through Hasek's pads for a 2-0 Swedish lead.

Jiri Dopita finally broke Salo's hex as he collected his own rebound off a right side rush and lifted the puck over the Swedish netminder at 10:23.

The final period featured more penalties, with the Czech Republic's Martin Havlat ejected from the game for boarding and Sundin taking two consecutive minors. Although the Czechs again outshot Sweden by a margin of 12-4 and exerted tremendous pressure, they were unable to get the goal they needed.

DAY 10

CANADA 3
CZECH 3

February 18   **Men**
4:10 p.m.   **E-Center**

There were enough plots and intrigue in a single hockey game this afternoon between Canada and the Czechs that the excitement of the play and the 3-3 result were almost entirely forgotten minutes after the final bell.

As in the Sweden game, Canada drew first blood when Mario Lemieux, back in the lineup, took a long pass from Scott Niedermayer, walked in on the Dominator and scored five-hole.

"It doesn't matter what we've done so far. After today, everything is important."
JOE SAKIC

But, as in that first game, Canada surrendered the 1-0 lead late in the period on a goal by Martin Havlat.

In the second, Havlat scored again after Eric Lindros failed to clear the puck out over his blueline. Havlat played on a line with Jaromir Jagr and Robert Lang, and the three were matched successfully by coach Josef Augusta against the Lindros line much of the night. Play then continued until the 18:49 mark of the middle period when all hell broke loose. Lemieux came down the right side on a two-on-one with Paul Kariya, and given the fact that he likely possesses the most accurate shot in the history of the game, he wasn't about to toss a pass over.

Hasek stopped the shot, but the momentum of his falling backward took him into his own goal. Was it a goal? The

"I play every day in New Jersey so I always have it in my mind that I'm going to play. I was happy to get the start. My first goal was to play in the Olympics. This is an opportunity and I don't want to miss the boat."
MARTIN BRODEUR

"Maybe we played too hard and that's why we made some silly mistakes. The Olympics are special and most of us don't play together at home, be we're all Czech people so we want to win very badly."
DOMINIK HASEK

red light came on, the Canadian players raised their arms, and, of course, the Czechs protested. Referee Bill McCreary went over to the phone, and video review allowed the goal on three points of criteria. One, the puck was clearly seen entering Hasek's glove. Two, the glove clearly fell back across the goal line into the net. Three, Hasek's momentum was not caused by contact with any Canadian player. The game was tied at 2-2.

Lemieux played an excellent game beside, working with Kariya and Sakic and generating many of the team's 36 shots. "I was skating better because I was at centre and I could use the ice more instead of just standing by the boards," he acknowledged. "And, any time you can get an extra day off at this time of year is also helpful."

Three minutes into the third period, Martin Brodeur made the save of the tournament when he lunged back to block a certain goal on a one-timer from a pass across the middle. (One interesting sidelight that was almost lost among

"We were trying to win the game. I think we outplayed them, to be honest. Look at the shots on goal. The three goals they scored, we gave them."
THEO FLEURY

the greater stories was the fact that Ed Belfour dressed as Brodeur's back-up, leaving Curtis Joseph in the stands.)

Nonetheless, Jiri Dopita scored at 13:17 of the third to give the Czechs the lead, but Canada rallied to tie the game on a great batting of the puck by Joe Nieuwendyk from a Fleury pass inches off the ice. Just a few moments later, though, Roman Hamrlik cross-checked Theo Fleury.

After the game, Wayne Gretzky went on a tear unlike any since he first played the game for real. "If that had been a Canadian player doing something like that to a European, the first thing I'd be asked by you guys [reporters] was whether he should be suspended, how Canadian players are hooligans. But the other way around, no one says anything. I'm so tired of people taking shots at Canadian hockey. I think that guy should be suspended for the rest of the tournament. The only thing about tournaments in this day and age is that we all play together. I sure think that Rangers-Islanders game next week is going to be interesting." [Hamrlik plays for the Islanders, Fleury and Lindros for the Rangers]

Pat Quinn voiced similar sentiments. "If something like that happens in the NHL, a guy can respond by beating the crap out of him. I tell my guys not to respond here. There will be a more appropriate time. One week from now, we'll get payback."

Rarely has Gretzky been so animated and impassioned by one game or series of events. "People don't understand the pressure the players are under," he continued.

"We don't care about Canada. We don't take them as the team to beat. I don't think they're the best team out there right now."
MARTIN RUCINSKY

"And people have no idea how much the other countries hate us and want to beat us. I know because they used to tell me on the ice all the time. The only people who want us

to win are the players and the Canadian fans."

"The expectations for our team are greater than any other team in the tournament. We had a very emotional game tonight, and the last goal gave us something to carry into the next game."

Gretzky's seventh-player emotions and the physical dominance of the team bode well for Canada's quarter-finals match against Finland on Wednesday. His reactions to the spear—as well as numerous hooking, slashing, and other third-period

Players from both teams land on top of Czech goalie Dominik Hasek as he makes the save off Mario Lemieux while falling back. The play went to video review, and Lemieux was awarded a goal when officials determined Hasek fell beyond the red line of his own will.

stick infractions by the Czechs— perhaps galvanized a team looking for an identity and a purpose and a pride. "If we did all that crap that they did tonight, we'd be goons, hooligans. We don't know how to play the game, we're animals. But when they do it, no one says a word,' he expanded.

On Wednesday, we would see just what effect today's on-ice events would have on the Canadians when they played Finland in the quarter-finals of the elimination round. ❧

Jarome Iginla works his way in front while being hounded by two Czechs.

Eloranta scored in the second for Finland, and another goal by Jere Lehtinen just 33 seconds into the third gave them a 3-1 lead they never relinquished. After the game, Russian journalists criticized their team's motivation, focus, and intensity. One asked if Bure agreed that the team had played as if it were "deaf and dumb" at times. Bure disagreed. "Even though we won, I'm even more happy with the way we were working on the ice tonight," said Finnish head coach Hannu Aravirta. "Because of the loss to the USA and the easy game against Belarus, we were a little unsure about how things are really for our team. This was good for our self-confidence." ❦

February 18	Men
FINLAND 3	RUSSIA 1
1:30 p.m.	The Peaks

some revenge for the 4-3 and 7-4 losses Russia had dealt them in Nagano by powering to a decisive 3-1 win. Teemu Selanne and Mikko

Early on, Finland let Russian sniper Pavel Bure roam all over the ice and the Finns paid a price when he powered between Aki-Petteri Berg and Ossi Vaananen and scored on a breakaway. "We started this game like we did against the USA," said Finnish defenseman Kimmo Timonen. "We gave them too much respect and we were standing still in the neutral zone. We talked about it in the first intermission and said, 'Come on, let's put the puck in deep and start skating and hitting their guys.'" The strategy worked, as the Finns got

February 18   **Men**
SWEDEN 7   **GERMANY 1**
7 p.m.   **The Peaks**

It was a battle of backup goalies at The Peaks this night as Sweden thrashed Germany 7-1 in its last final round game. Johan Hedberg went between the pipes for Sweden, giving Tommy Salo the night off. "I realized right away this was going to be an easy night when we got a 3-0 lead," said Hedberg. "I just tried to keep sharp and keep my body working." Markus Naslund scored twice for Sweden, while Mats Sundin, Mikael Renberg, Mathias Johansson, Daniel Alfredsson and Tomas Holmstrom scored for Sweden. Dennis Seidenberg replied for Germany. Sweden had already clinched top spot in Group C before the game and Germany was stuck in fourth, so this merely served as a tuneup for playoff round action for both teams. Tre Kronor looked ahead to what looked to be an easy game versus Belarus on Wednesday, while the Germans prepared to meet the USA. Daniel Alfredsson sounded a note of caution for his Swedish teammates. "We know that Belarus has some skilled players. We have to come out from the first faceoff and play hard," said Alfredsson. It was a good thought at the time.

February 18   **Men**
USA 8   **BELARUS 1**
11 a.m.   **E-Center**

Vladimir Tsyplakov of Belarus took the puck from the opening faceoff and moved into U.S. territory down the right wing. He circled the net, passed back to the point, took a quick return pass, and whipped the puck to Dmitry Pankov alone in the slot. Pankov drilled the disc past starter Tom Barrasso, and after 20 seconds Belarus held a 1-0 lead. The final score in the game was 8-1 USA, a score that flattered Belarus, save for the exceptional goaltending of Andrei Mezin who faced 48 shots, easily half of which were excellent chances.

"We didn't have the start to the game that we wanted," Tony Amonte said, though teammate Brett Hull summed up the game accurately when he commented that, "He [Mezin] just kept making save after save and stoned us, but we knew when we got one, they'd start to come."

The quick first goal helped open the game, but throughout the first period Mezin stopped an incredible 15 shots, almost every one in close. The Belarussians escaped that period with a 1-0 lead, but in the second the Americans continued to press and wore Mezin down. Hull scored on what must have been his "fifteenth shot," but still the score after two was a respectable 3-1.

When the United States scored again early in the third, the Belarus team gave up the ghost. The players stopped skating, and the defence stopped defending, and Mezin was left to tend his end of the ice virtually alone. But for him, the Americans would have hit double digits comfortably.

Perhaps most impressive about the American team is how well they've played as a team so quickly, an achievement Brooks attributes mostly to Chris Chelios. "It's really his team" he noted. "He's a tremendous leader, with what he says, what he does. And this is a guy who's forty years old. He's not a kid. I've talked to him once a week all season about the team." The other quality the team is demonstrating is an ability to score and create scoring chances. ❦

DAY
11

CANADA 7
FINLAND 3

February 19   Women
11:05 a.m.   E-Center

"There is no finals if you don't play the semi-finals well," Isabelle Chartrand said after a tight 7-3 Canadian win over Finland today to advance to the gold medal game.

For almost 20 minutes of today's game the Finns held a 3-2 lead. But there was no panic on the Canadian bench, only confidence. "We knew if we just kept on them the goals would come," Hayley Wickenheiser said. She was right in spades. Canada trailed to start the third, but poured it on in the early going by setting a women's Olympic record with goals just six seconds apart by Wickenheiser to tie the game and Jayna Hefford to win it. The team added three more before time expired, but the players knew the 7-3 score was much closer.

"Finland is just a step away," Cassie Campbell said afterward. "I think they're a team that could very easily have been in the gold medal game, even in Nagano. I think it's just an attitude change that they have to have and someone's got to step up and make it."

Coming off the ice, the Canadian women shouted to each other, "Nice comeback!" in the corridors, but it wasn't their lack of effort that had caused the minor blip in their smooth performance here at Salt Lake. Canada outshot the Finns 54-18, and were it not for the outstanding goaltending of Tuula Puputti the score would have been much higher. Rarely did the Finns have sustained pressure in the Canadian end, and their two second-period goals to take the lead were the result of lightning-quick strikes that saw the Canadian defence caught flat-footed ever so briefly.

The Finns scored late in the first to halve a 2-0 Canadian lead. It was the first goal Sami Jo Small has given up here, ending her shutout streak at 199:35. Canada continued to

GAME SUMMARY

First Period

1	Canada, Brisson (unassisted)	5:58
2	Canada, Wickenheiser (Chartrand)	8:10
3	Finland, Reima (Fisk, Riipi)	19:35

penalties: Salo (Fin)	4:02
Sunohara (Can)	7:38
Kellar (Can)	10:39
Sostorics (Can) & Laaksonen (Fin)	16:21

Second Period

4	Finland, Reima (Fisk, Hanninen)	2:56
5	Finland, Riipi (Reima, Fisk)	3:51

penalties: Sunohara (Can)	4:30
Vaarakallio (Fin)	8:33
Sirvio (Fin)	10:15
Sirvio (Fin)	13:21
Salo (Fin)	18:15

Third Period

6	Canada, Wickenheiser (Goyette, St. Pierre)	3:19
7	Canada, Hefford (Sunohara)	3:25
8	Canada, Sunohara (Goyette)	17:26
9	Canada, Campbell (unassisted)	18:32
10	Canada, Brisson (Botterill)	19:03

penalties: Palvila (Fin)	18:46

In Goal

CANADA	Kim St. Pierre
FINLAND	Tuula Puputti

Shots on Goal

CANADA	18	22	14	54
FINLAND	7	6	5	18

Referee	Stacey Livingston
Linesmen	Megan Mackenzie
	Julie Piacentini

Action from Canada's 7-3 win over Finland in the women's semi-finals. (top) Finland's Satu Hoikkala goes for a spill. (middle) Canada's Hayley Wickenheiser is tied up behind the Finnish goal. (below) Canada's women celebrate the team's final goal.

dominate, but Puputti made several great saves, none larger than one on a Lori Dupuis breakaway in the second. Brisson and Wickenheiser both had two goals, the others credited to Hefford, Sunohara, and Campbell.

The importance of the game was highlighted by the oddest of events in a women's game—pushing and shoving after the whistle. Players on both teams went to the net and refused to slow down as they reached the crease, and the defence was unusually aggressive in protecting its goalie from aggressive forwards.

The women and their families joined the Canadian men's team for dinner and a combined team portrait. On Thursday came the inevi-

table gold medal game against the United States. Although Canada has won each and every one of the seven world championships played, it has lost the one most coveted game, the 1998 gold medal at Nagano. Additionally, the Americans had beaten Canada in their past eight exhibition games leading up to Salt Lake.

"We're happy with the way we played in those games," Vicky Sunohara said of that disastrous exhibition schedule. "But," she added, "we have a lot of respect for them."

"I don't think we have to do anything differently. The pressure is on them. They're defending Olympic champion and they're playing in their own barn," Campbell opined.

"We're just going to have to play our best game to beat them. What happened in Nagano — not to take anything away from them—is that we didn't execute as much as we would have liked to. They had nothing to lose going into that game, but we're kind of in that position this time around."

"We're going to have to play really defensive to win that gold medal," Isabelle Chartrand said after. "We also have to make sure we capitalize on the offense on the chances we get."

''I kind of think the U.S. is going to win this round, but they also have to find a way to score," goalie Puputti offered.

#99 STANDS BY HIS WORDS

Wayne Gretzky held a press conference today and offered no apology and expressed no regret for venting after last night's 3-3 tie with the Czechs. He reiterated his belief that every team wants to beat Canada because it is a particularly treasured feather in any country's cap. "I have no regrets about what I said. I simply said it was a penalty, blatant, and that other countries love to beat us. I have nothing against Roman Hamrlik," he began, "I've known him since he was 18 years old. All I'm saying is what I said yesterday— if a Canadian did it, that's the first thing everyone would want to talk about."

"I'm proud of our team. The last straw was when I heard that Mario had gone home," he said, trying to explain what caused his outburst and just how incensed he was by inflammatory rumours about the team captain's departure. "I was speaking from the heart. I felt like our team was getting bombarded and I was just trying to stand up for our hockey club."

Gretzky confirmed that Mario Lemieux's injury remains his hip and nothing else. He also said, "it's highly unlikely there will be a change" in goaltenders (i.e., Brodeur would start) and said Ed Belfour dressed as backup last night because the team wanted to make him feel part of the contingent. Needless to say, this comes at the expense of Curtis Joseph, who might find himself in the stands for the remainder of the Olympics after his performance in the first game.

As for his role as manager and not player, Gretzky offered a wonderful anecdote. "I remember game three. I stayed at my parents' house in Hamilton in 1987 (during the Canada Cup), and I got up and my dad drove to the rink with me. I remember seeing how nervous he was and how much he was pacing. I remember asking him why he was so nervous and told him not to be worried. When you played, it's a different kind of worry. You go in the dressing room and you get ready for the game and you get excited about it and you go on the ice and you do it. It was the most fun you could ever have. Watching is awfully tough. It's very emotional."

As for all direct questions about the team itself, the game, the makeup, Gretzky had just one thing to say: "We play tomorrow night." By that time, his team would be either on a roll or on a bus out of town.

February 19　　　Women
RUSSIA 5　　　GERMANY 0
7 p.m.　　　　The Peaks

Russia completed its 2002 women's Olympic tournament on a solid note with a 5-0 win over Germany in placement game action. Tatiana Burina led the way with two first-period goals, while other Russian scores came from Tatiana Tsareva, Ekaterina Smolentseva, and Svetlana Trefilova. Goaltender Irina Gashennikova made 25 saves to earn her first shutout. Her final GAA of 2.40 and save percentage of .932 ranked fourth behind Sara DeCosta of the USA, Kim St. Pierre of Canada, and Kim Martin of Sweden. The result gave Russia fifth place and the Germans, sixth.

❦

February 19　　　Women
CHINA 2　　　KAZAKHSTAN 1
2 p.m.　　　　The Peaks

It took overtime to settle this tightly-played affair, which featured 35 shots on goal from both China and Kazakhstan. Hongmei Liu emerged as the hero, beating Kazakhstan's Natalya Trunova 1:39 into the fourth period. China's other goal came from Xiuqing Yang. Nadezhda Losyeva had the only goal for Kazakhstan, scoring with just 2:14 left in regulation time. The victory secured seventh place in the final tournament standings for China, while the Kazakhs fell to eighth spot. Overall, it was disappointing finish for the Chinese, who had outperformed both Sweden and Japan to claim fourth place at the Nagano Olympics back in 1998.

February 19　　　Women
USA 4　　　SWEDEN 0
4:30 p.m.　　　E-Center

USA Secretary of Defense Donald Rumsfeld was among the spectators for this well-attended semi-finals matchup, which saw the USA dominate from start to finish. However, defense was the key to the victory, not offense. The 32-10 shots on goal total favouring the USA was less than one might have anticipated. But the Swedes weren't able to capitalize on any of their meager chances, and that was what mattered for coach Ben Smith's crew, who pushed the USA's all-time record versus Sweden to 18-0.

Cammi Granato emerged as the offensive leader for the USA, scoring two goals and an assist in the win. Katie King and Natalie Darwitz had the other American scores, while Tara Mounsey and Krissy Wendell recorded two assists apiece. After the game, Smith announced he would start Sara DeCosta in the gold medal game, even though Sarah Tueting picked up this win. "The decision's already made," said Smith. "I rotate my goalies." At the 1998 Olympics, where gold went to the USA, Tueting had played in both the semi-finals and the finals. Evidently, Smith wasn't worried about changing his team's luck.

DAY 12

CANADA 2
FINLAND 1

February 20	Men
8:15 p.m.	E-Center

Canada has done it. Pat Quinn asked for three games to get his team ready, and tonight, three games later, they were ready, defeating Finland 2-1 in a tough, sometimes dirty, NHL-style game. "We've been getting better every game, but I still think there's more there," Quinn said after.

"They forechecked really hard with two or three guys and put lots of pressure on us," Scott Niedermayer noted, "and we clogged up the middle." As a result, the no-red line rule became a moot point over the course of the evening.

"We gave them too much room and they were able to score. We battled back, but it wasn't enough," Kimmo Timonen observed.

As with the team's previous game against the Czechs, Wayne Gretzky sat on the team's player bench during the pre-game skate, perhaps for both pride and intimidation.

Canada scored the first goal of the game for the fourth straight time, and for the third time it was an early score that gave them the 1-0 lead when Joe Sakic put a backhand between Jani Hurme's pads from a bad angle. But unlike the quick scores against Sweden and the Czechs, they escaped the first period with the lead by playing NHL-style hockey. There were no concerns about the long pass—using it or defending it—and they both dumped the puck in and also forced Finland to do the same.

"Our job was to keep going at it.

GAME SUMMARY

First Period

1 Canada, Sakic (Gagne)　　　　3:00
penalties: none

Second Period

2 Canada, Yzerman (Lemieux)　　15:49
3 Finland, Hagman (Kallio, Jokinen)16:09
penalties: Selanne (Can)　　　　5:52

Third Period

No Scoring
penalties: Jovanovski (Can)　　　6:10

In Goal

FINLAND	Jani Hurme
CANADA	Martin Brodeur

Shots on Goal

FINLAND	5	8	6	19
CANADA	15	14	5	34

Referee	Dennis LaRue
Linesmen	Mike Cvik/Rudolf Lauff

"I'm having a blast. Every time I go out to play, I hope to go out and contribute. Definitely I expected to play. If you get the chance or not it is out of my control. It is my chance to lead Canada and win some medals here it would be something great. It is a lot of fun. Now that we are in the middle of the tournament, I hope we will keep it going."

"They had a few opportunities to come at me and I don't know what they were doing. We were able to counter because of it. They were making drop pass after drop pass. Our second goal came because of this. They weren't really shooting the puck that much."
MARTIN BRODEUR

"All the guys on our team have great hockey sense and can adapt to different situations. We've made adjustments and improved every game. We were gearing everything towards tonight. I thought we played real well defensively."
THEO FLEURY

We had a lot of chances, but we had only a one-goal lead," said Niedermayer.

The second period was more of the same. Canada's defence stood the Finns up at the blueline, and Martin Brodeur was solid if unspectacular in goal. Canada had a number of excellent scoring chances from the defence but couldn't hit the net to save their lives. Once again, it was Super Mario who made the play of the period when he took a pass on a three-on-two. As he cut from the left into the middle, Kariya steamed to the net. Lemieux then calmly passed against the flow to Yzerman who

Canadian goalie Martin Brodeur celebrates victory after his team's narrow 2-1 win over the Finns in the quarter-finals to earn a semi-finals date with the Belarussians who stunned the Swedes 4-3.

had an empty net. Canada 2-0. "I though he was going to shoot," Yzerman admitted, "but I had an empty net in front of me."

On the ensuing shift, however, the Finns came right back and Niklas Hagman scored with a low shot to the glove side from in close. The goal gave the Finns some much-needed confidence for the third, but Canada's defence was impenetrable for most of the night. The team allowed just 19 shots, and Brodeur was efficient in goal.

In large part Canada was allowed to play its style because of the officiating of NHLer Dennis LaRue who "let 'em play," as the saying goes, allowing more clutching and grabbing and interference and stickwork than a European official might have. He called Selanne for goaltender interference in the second and Ed Jovanovski in the third, but besides that he pocketed the whistle and let the players decide the game.

As usual, there was always a story behind the story. Eric Lindros was benched the last half of the game, and it wasn't due to any health problems. "We got into a groove with the people we were using and decided to go with those players," Pat Quinn said after.

The question now was one of psychology as Friday's semi-finals game against Belarus approached. Was that underdog team content with its victory over Sweden to the point it would play down to its former self? Would Canada play flat, thinking the game was won before it had been played? Could Canada maintain high emotion as it had tonight for a team that has never challenged it? Could the Belarussians pull another incredible performance out of its hockey bag? "They beat a tremendous team who beat us," Niedermayer said. [A letdown] is not an option." ✤

NOTES

Coach Pat Quinn used the following combinations. Up front: Sakic, Gagne, Iginla; Yzerman, Kariya, Lemieux; Nolan, Lindros, Smyth; Nieuwendyk, Fleury, Shanahan. On defence: MacInnis and Pronger; Foote and Niedermayer; Blake and Jovanovski. Eric Brewer did not dress. Finnish coach Hannu Aravirta used the following forward combinations: Selanne, Lehtinen, Aalto; Eloranta, Kapanen, Ylonen; Jokinen, Hagman, Kallio; Helminen, Ruutu, Lind. On defence: Timonen and Numminen; Berg and Lumme; Niinimaa and Salo; and, Vaananen as seventh defenceman ... Canada wore white and Finland blue ... during the ceremonial pennant exchange, Mario Lemieux forgot to shake hands with the referee and linesmen; Teemu Selanne, more comfortable with international custom, perhaps, didn't make the same mistake.

February 20   **Men**
BELARUS 4   **SWEDEN 3**
11 a.m.   **E-Center**

This qualified as one of the most stunning upsets in Olympic hockey history, comparable only with the 1980 "Miracle on Ice" and Great Britain's 2-1 win over Canada in the 1936 Olympic Winter Games. Vladimir Kopat scored the winner on a freaky shot with 2:24 remaining in the third period (see photo p.63, bottom). Coming down the right wing, he slapped a high shot from between the red line and blue line toward Swedish goalie Tommy Salo, who didn't know how to handle it. The puck hit Salo in the mask area, bounced off his head and trickled over the goal line. "I feel bad for Team Sweden," said Belarus goalie Andrei Mezin, who stood on his head to stop 44 of 47 Swedish shots.

Early in the game, Swedish goalie Tommy Salo demonstrates a confidence with the puck that betrayed him at the crucial moment of his semi-finals game against Belarus.

Daniel Alfredsson is stopped by Andrei Mezin on a good chance in close.

Belarus goalie Andrei Mezin covers up while Tomas Holmstrom looks for a loose puck.

After beating Tommy Salo with just 2:24 to go in the game, Belarus's Vladimir Kopat dives headlong toward his bench where his teammates mob their hero.

"I really like them. I expected them to go to the final or the top four. For sure it's a miracle for us." Belarus head coach Vladimir Krikunov said he had lost a bottle of cognac in a bet over the result of the game. Sweden had gone a perfect 3-0 in the final round with convincing wins over Canada, the Czech Republic, and Germany, while Belarus was 0-3 with 22 goals allowed in losses to Russia, Finland, and the USA. But none of that mattered now. "It's devastating," said Sweden's Markus Naslund. "It's the toughest loss I've had so far in my hockey career." "Sometimes even a gun without bullets shoots, and that was us today," Mezin explained with poetic brilliance. ❦

February 20
RUSSIA 1
1:30 p.m.

Men
CZECH 0
The Peaks

The Dominator was out-Dominated today as Russia eliminated three-time world champions and Olympics title holders from the Czech Republic with a stifling 1-0 win. Although the game could not compete with the extraordinary events that took place at the E-Center earlier when the Belarussians eliminated Sweden 4-3, this was a tense game nonetheless.

The first period was scoreless, but the Russians drew first, and only, blood in the second off a faceoff. A slapshot from the point hit a Czech defenceman in front and the puck bounced at the feet of Maxim Afinogenov who batted it past Dominik Hasek.

A short time later, Nikolai Khabibulin made a great save off Robert Lang during a Czech power play when he slid across the crease to block a shot. Alexei Kovalev then had a clear breakaway, and as Hasek fell, Kovalev snapped a shot above the goalie's pads only to see the puck hit the crossbar. The exact same thing occurred at the other end when Jiri Dopita hit the iron on a power play for the Czechs.

The third period began the way much of the second was played. The Russians were disciplined on defence and blocked shots and passes to perfection. But midway through, the Czechs opened the game up at long last, creating numerous scoring chances only to be stopped by the Bulin Wall. Martin Havlat hit the post on one rush, and the goalie stopped Robert Lang point blank with his glove on another occasion.

The Czechs did not pull Hasek until there were but 15 seconds left in the game, but on the rush, Jaromir Jagr passed the puck out front and a wild scramble ensued, both Petr Sykora and Lang getting phenomenal chances with fewer than ten seconds left.

The victory paved way for a possible Russia-USA rematch of a few days ago, a 2-2 tie that was the best game of these Olympics to date for skill and entertainment.

February 20　　　　　**Men**
USA 5　　　　　**GERMANY 0**
4 p.m.　　　　　**E-Center**

The USA dispatched the upstart Germans with ease in the second quarter-finals at the E-Center. The Germans took far too many penalties, including a couple of high-sticks to John LeClair's face. "When you play the U.S., you have to be fully concentrated for 60 minutes," said German head coach Hans Zach. "The referee is not to be blamed for our loss." The USA got some revenge for its last Olympic meeting with the Germans, a 4-3 loss in Lillehammer in 1994. The Americans admitted they had received motivation from the Belarus upset of Sweden. "The Belarus thing added more momentum, a wake-up call," said USA head coach Herb Brooks. "This is not a chess game on ice. It's about character and commitment, doing the things you need to do to stay alive." Mike

Richter earned his first shutout of the tournament with 28 saves. In the post-game press conference, Brooks revealed that Keith Tkachuk was questionable for the

upcoming semi-finals versus Russia because of a groin injury, while Doug Weight had missed the third period against Germany due to flu.　　🍁

DAY 13

GOLD MEDAL GAME

CANADA 3
USA 2

February 21 **Women**
5:10 p.m. **E-Center**

A couple of days ago, Hayley Wickenheiser more or less announced that the Americans' success in recent months was a self-fulfilling prophecy for failure in Salt Lake City. She said the Americans would wilt under pressure of expectations to win gold on home turf. Today, she contributed to a correct prediction with a vital goal in the second period to lead Canada to a 3-2 win over the USA.

Early in the game, she said, "I could see the fear [of those expectations] in their eyes."

"She's a great player, not an optometrist," United States coach Ben Smith replied after learning of Wickenheiser's remarks. Nonetheless, the Americans did wilt under that pressure. After defeating Canada eight consecutive times in the pre-Olympic months, the team simply was outplayed in the game, despite having eight power plays in a row during one stretch.

"They beat us with it, that's for sure," Vicky Sunohara acknowledged of the effective U.S. power play in recent months, "but we made some adjustments and Kim [St. Pierre] played phenomenal goal for us." Smith agreed. "The key to killing penalties is goaltending," he admitted.

Cammi Granato, the cog in the American power play, also realized how important the power play was. "The key to

First Period

1 Canada, Ouellette (Piper)		1:45
penalties: Looney (USA)		6:17
Kennedy (USA)		10:54
Botterill (Can)		12:15
Wickenheiser (Can)		14:05
Brisson (Can)		17:01
Sunohara (Can)		17:52

Second Period

2 USA, King (Granato, Mounsey)		1:59
3 Canada, Wickenheiser (Goyette)		4:10
4 Canada, Hefford (Kellar, Brisson)		19:59
penalties: Kellar (Can)		1:11
Ouellette (Can)		4:51
Chartrand (Can)		11:25
Botterill (Can)		14:03
Wendell (USA)		15:37
Kennedy (USA) & Ouellette (Can)		18:05

Third Period

5 USA, Bye (Mounsey, Potter)		16:27
penalties: Wall (USA)		0:44
Kellar (Can)		1:49
Sostorics (Can)		5:02
Baker (USA) & Dupuis (Can)		10:56
Bechard (Can)		16:04

In Goal

USA	Sara Decosta
CANADA	Kim St. Pierre

Shots on Goal

USA	11	9	7	27
CANADA	9	10	10	29

Referee	Stacey Livingston
Linesmen	Johanna Suban
	Henrieta Hujdusova

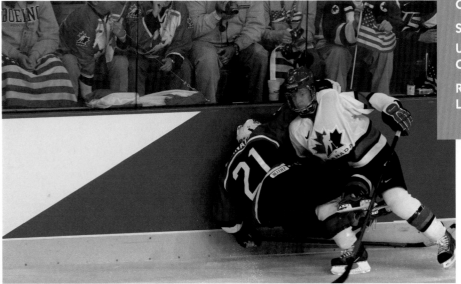

"I knew from day one what to expect from the U.S. It was just a matter of us playing 60 minutes, and that's something we haven't done all year."
DANIELE SAUVAGEAU

playing them [Canada] is the specialty teams and we certainly had our chances. Today, we didn't put them in. Indeed, the United States had a staggering eleven power plays in the game, including two separate five-on-three situations. They scored both their goals with the extra player, but two-of-eleven is still not good enough to win. In fact, the United States had a total of 15:52 power play time to just 6:00 for Canada.

"We know each other's tendencies," Smith began. "In the early going, we pressed a bit on the power play. We had a couple of open nets we didn't hit, and then I think it be-

came a matter of having too many power plays." Both Granato and Jenny Potter had perfect set-ups to score on open nets in the first period, and both times they gripped the stick too tightly and missed badly. They were on their heels from early on when Caroline Ouellette scored for Canada just 1:45 into the game. Although the United States had some eight minutes in power play time in the opening 20 minutes, the period ended 1-0 Canada.

The man advantage was key to United States success during that eight-game tour. They had eleven goals with the extra man and Canada had but two. If they had maintained this advantage, they

Canada's women celebrate their dramatic 3-2 win over USA to claim gold at the Salt Lake 2002 Olympic Winter Games.

would almost certainly have won the game. Without it, they lost one of their great weapons.

Case in point: early in the second, Canada was called for another penalty by referee Stacey Livingston, and 48 seconds later Katie King tipped in a point shot beautifully to tie the game. But the Americans let their guard down and, just two minutes later, Canada took the lead again on a nice effort by Hayley Wickenheiser. That was the first turning point in the game. The next came with 13 seconds left in the period. With a faceoff in the Canadian end, the United States lost the draw and Therese Brisson hit Jayna Hefford with a long pass. She went in on a breakaway, was stopped by Sara DeCosta, but knocked in the rebound with just one second left in the period (see photo below). Canada entered the dressing room leading 3-1 with just 20 minutes to play.

That made a comeback for the Americans all the tougher in the third, and Canada played defence with a poise and determination equal to the importance of the game. The United States had three more power plays, but didn't score until 16:27 on another shot from the blueline by Karyn Bye that went in untipped this time. In the dying minutes, the Canadians put up a net, a wall, and a blanket all to deny U.S. entry into their end of the ice.

"It was a great experience to play at the Olympics at home. The crowd was behind us 100 per cent," Granato said. "Any time that you don't reach what you want to do, it's disappointing. We did everything that we could to prepare. We have a lot to be proud of, but Canada came out and played a great game. It was our goal to win this tournament, but it was Canada's, too, and they came out on top." ❧

Canadian players mob goalie Kim St. Pierre at the end of their incredible 3-2 win over the heavily-favoured USA in the women's gold medal game.

Colleen Sostorics breaks down during the medals presentation.

February 21 — **Women**
BRONZE MEDAL GAME
SWEDEN 2 — FINLAND 1
12:00 p.m. — The Peaks

Two months ago, the Swedish Olympic Federation wanted to renege on its signed agreement with the IOC to send its women's hockey team to Salt Lake. It argued that the team's horrible results during the exhibition season in preparation for the 2002 Olympics indicated that it couldn't compete, and that it would be a waste of time to send the girls to play. The Federation didn't take into account that the team played only Canada, Finland, and the United States, the strongest teams in the world.

Today, Sweden, led by 15-year-old goalie Kim Martin, stunned Finland 2-1 to win bronze. The Swedes now have salvaged something from their hockey here in Salt Lake, but for the Finns it was their second consecu-tive day of elimination, the men having been sent home by Canada yesterday after a 2-1 loss.

Sweden scored early when Gunilla Andersson stepped in over the blueline and wired a shot that goalie Puputti got a blocker on. The rebound came right to Evelina Samuelsson and she bounced the puck into the open side. The goal seemed to ignite the Finns and they took to the attack for the next few minutes. However, they were stopped by some fine goaltending and a Swedish defence that blocked shots and intercepted passes effectively.

Finland's momentum was check-ed by two successive penalties, the second of which cost them another goal on a wild scramble in front. Puputti made several saves but couldn't freeze the puck, and even-tually Samuelsson again pushed in the loose disc for a 2-0 Sweden lead through the first period.

Hanne Sikio brought the Finns within one on a goal midway through the second, but despite three more power plays they couldn't even the score. That was how the rest of the game went. Finland outshot Sweden 33-20 in what was a superb goaltender's battle, but Suomi could not beat Martin. She stopped breakaways, one-tim-ers, pretty dekes and long slap shots, and her defence blocked many more shots that might have been dangerous.

For Finland, bronze medallists in 1998, a lack of scoring cost the team a 2002 medal. More to the point, the Finns were scoreless in eight chances on the power play. In the third, they had tremendous oppor-tunities but simply couldn't score. And so, while the Finns pack their bags and the Swedish Olympic Fed-eration hides in embarrassment, the Swedish women celebrated their historic medal.   ❦

DAY 14

CANADA 7
BELARUS 1

February 22   Men
12:00 p.m.   E-Center

Canada posted a big 7-1 victory over Belarus to advance to the gold medal game of the men's hockey tournament. The Canadians will face the winner of the USA-Russia semi-finals in the glamour event of these Olympics. "It was important for us to win by a big margin," said captain Mario Lemieux.

"We're not satisfied. We expected to be here. One more game to go. Whoever we play, we'll have to be at our best. We can't worry about the expectation. We just have to play our game the best we can."
JOE SAKIC

Steve Yzerman led Canada with a goal and two assists, while Eric Brewer, Scott Niedermayer, Paul Kariya, Simon Gagne, Eric Lindros, and Jarome Iginla each scored once. Lemieux had two assists and NHLer Ruslan Salei had the lone tally for Belarus.

Canada outshot Belarus 51-14 and scored four more goals than it had in any previous contest at the 2002 Games. Belarus had to gear up for its final game the next night against the other semi-finals loser, Russia.

"We still have a chance for a bronze medal, and I think it's great," said Belarus goalie Andrei Mezin. "We're still gonna fight." Meanwhile, a Canadian win on February 24 would give the red and white its

GAME SUMMARY

First Period

1	Canada, Yzerman (Sakic, Blake)		6:05
2	Belarus, Salei (unassisted)		13:25
3	Canada, Brewer (Yzerman)		17:25
penalties: Kopat (Bel)			1:52
Fleury (Can) & Mikulchik (Bel)			16:05

Second Period

4	Canada, Niedermayer (Lemieux, Kariya)		2:09
5	Canada, Kariya (Yzerman, Lemieux)		13:28
penalties: Kovalev (Bel)			1:10
Jovanovski (Can)			2:38
Peca (Can)			5:11
Mikulchik (Bel)			9:59

Third Period

6	Canada, Gagne (Peca)		5:21
7	Canada, Lindros (Smyth, Nolan)		12:24
8	Canada, Iginla (Shanahan)		16:15
penalties: Niedermayer (Can)			3:31
Fleury (Can)			6:56
Nolan (Can)			8:43
(Bel-too many men)			10:52
Lindros (Can) & Tsyplakov (Bel)			17:43
Lindros (Can) & Tsyplakov (Bel)			19:54

In Goal

CANADA	Martin Brodeur
BELARUS	Andrei Mezin

Shots on Goal

CANADA	17	15	19	51
BELARUS	3	6	5	14

Referee	Stephen Walkom
Linesmen	Sergei Kulakov/Tim Nowak

first gold medal in men's hockey since the 1952 Olympics in Oslo, Norway.

An enthusiastic group of fans wearing Team Canada sweaters from the 1972 Summit Series took their seats to the right of Belarus goaltender Andrei Mezin's net in the first period, cheering the favoured Canadian squad. The E-Center was packed with Canadian fans,

while a handful of Belarus supporters chanted their team's name from the upper deck.

Both teams came out with an aggressive, high tempo. Canada dominated territorially, not permitting Belarus a shot on goal until 10:10 into the game.

Canadian pressure in the offensive zone led to the first penalty against the Belarussians, as Vladimir Kopat was sent off at 3:52 for high-sticking. Al MacInnis almost capitalized on the ensuing man advantage, ringing a shot off the crossbar. Theoren Fleury rattled Mezin with a shot off his mask,

forcing a stoppage in play (an IIHF rule).

Steve Yzerman opened the scoring for Canada at 6:05, picking up Joe Sakic's rebound in the slot and beating Mezin. Ruslan Salei tied the game at 13:24 on Belarus's third shot of the game when Martin Brodeur bobbled the drive from just inside the blueline.

Canada intensified its efforts after the goal, to avoid suffering a fate similar to Team Sweden's embarrassing 4-3 loss to Belarus in the quarter-finals. Lemieux and Kariya fired tremendous shots at the Belarus net, but to no avail.

Nieuwendyk put one off the side of the net, and Mezin stared Fleury down from the left faceoff circle. Eric Brewer tried to replicate his solo effort from the game against Sweden, but Mezin prevented a goal with a nifty pokecheck.

Finally, Brewer converted a Steve Yzerman pass from behind the net at 17:25. Mezin made the initial save but pushed his right leg — and the puck — back over the red line.

Canada bounced one off the post with less than two minutes left in the opening period, and then Michael Peca came in off the right wing to backhand a shot off the

crossbar. The shots on goal in the first period favoured Canada 17-3.

With Andrei Kovalev in the penalty box for holding at 1:10 of the second, Canada capitalized on a neutral zone turnover when Lemieux came down left wing and centered the puck to Scott Niedermayer, who beat Mezin through the five-hole for a 3-1 lead. "In the second, we made some big mistakes and they capitalized on them and put the game away, pretty much," Salei commented.

Defenseman Oleg Khmyl broke up a potential two-on-one with Lemieux and Kariya and Lindros missed the net when he was set up all alone in the slot. Simon Gagne put a rebound from Joe Sakic's shot through the crease behind Mezin.

Canada didn't stop. Yzerman and Kariya then broke down on a two-on-one that Kariya converted with a rising shot that hit Mezin's pad and went up under the crossbar for a 4-1 lead at 13:28. "Stevie's a very smart player," said Lemieux. "He controls the puck very well and he's able to pick the open guy."

Immediately afterwards, Belarus coach Vladimir Krikunov pulled Mezin, replacing him with Sergei Shabanov.

With under two minutes left in the second, Ryan Smyth broke free for a shot off the inside of the right post, which Shabanov reached back to smother with his glove before the red light went on.

Canada faced a short-handed situation early in the third when Niedermayer was sent off for high-sticking. Belarus generated some decent chances off Khmyl's work at the point but was unable to score. When Oleg Antonenko lost the puck at the blueline, Peca was off to the races with Simon Gagne, who deked Shabanov on the backhand for Canada's fifth goal of the game at 5:21.

Belarus proved unable to score with the two-man advantage when Fleury and Nolan briefly shared the penalty box midway through the period. With 28 seconds remaining in a Belarus penalty for too many men on the ice, Lindros unleashed a heavy one-timer for his first goal and point of the tournament at 12:24, making the score 6-1.

Later, Brendan Shanahan dug out the puck along the boards and centred it to Iginla, who launched another one-timer for his first goal and point of the tournament at 16:15, rounding out the scoring for Canada. "A game like this was kind of nice for us to get some confidence out there, to get a goal here or there," said Al MacInnis. "It was nice to see the scoring spread around."

Lindros took a nasty slash at Vladimir Tsyplakov at 17:49 after the Belarus forward roughed him up in the corner, and both players headed to the penalty box. Lindros couldn't contain his impulse for vengeance and went after Tsyplakov again with six seconds left in the game. "It's an emotional game and it's the semi-finals, so we didn't expect anything different," Iginla said.

Canadian fans in their '72 sweaters were so excited about the prospect of going to the finals that they launched into an impromptu rendition of "O, Canada" in the last couple of minutes. They then chanted "Russia! Russia!" to indicate the opponent they would prefer to face in the finals. "Like in 1972, with Phil Esposito stepping up, everybody comes together as a team," said Ryan Smyth. "We've done that thus far and we want to continue with it."

Salei described how "outrageously happy" people in his country had phoned him and his family after the 4-3 win over Sweden, weeping as they spoke. "I think we made history for Belarus, and this story may not be repeated again," he said.

Canada, meanwhile, was just one step away from its own historic celebration. ♣

(left) Goalie Martin Brodeur celebrates a Canadian score during the team's easy 7-1 win in the semi-finals to advance to the gold medal game against the winner of the Russia-USA game that night. (above) Brodeur flags down a shot from the point.

Twenty-two years to the day that the USA defeated CCCP 4-3 to come within a game of a gold medal during the "Miracle on Ice" run at Lake Placid, Russians Slava Fetisov and Vladislav Tretiak lined up behind their bench as coaches to oppose Miracle coach Herb Brooks.

The result was a game of political and sporting intrigue that produced some utterly breathtaking hockey.

Chants of "USA! USA!" greeted the American team from the moment the players stepped on the ice.

Roused, they came out flying, outshooting Russia 20-4 and creating most of the scoring chances in the first period. Russia kept pace skating-wise, but couldn't penetrate the American blueline the way the red, white, and blue used its outside speed to close in on Nikolai Khabibulin time and again.

While the Russians demonstrated better individual speed, the Americans had better team speed. While the Russians were tougher on the puck, the Americans possessed a quick transition game. But the only goal of the period came on a power play with Andrei Nikolishin in the box for tripping. The USA had terrific possession, and a flurry around the net led to Bill Guerin smacking a loose puck over top of Khabibulin.

If the USA didn't establish itself with enough purpose in the first, it seemed to settle the game for certain in the second. The Americans got two more power play goals on almost identical plays. They maintained possession, peppered Khabibulin, and knocked in rebounds in a scramble from close range. By about the midway point, the Russians virtually gave up. They avoided physical contact, veered away from the net, and made no effort to establish any sort of an offensive game. Coach Fetisov called a time out, but it had no effect in either picking up his team or calming down the Americans. After two periods, shots were 38-11, and none of those dozen-less-one were particularly difficult for Mike Richter.

What happened in the third period was the most extraordinary turn of events of this tournament that produced the most thrilling, dramatic, fiercest period of hockey the city of Salt Lake likely has ever seen. A simple shoot-in by the Russians to start the period bounced right in front of the net and Andrei Kovalev put the puck between Mike Richter's legs just eleven seconds into the final period. The Russians continued an unbelievably relentless attack, and at 3:21 a point shot went through Richter's legs again. 3-2. Incredible.

"We were sort of scrambling for a while," Brian Leetch said. "They didn't quit and they have a lot of character. I think Mikey [Richter] made some big saves for us and we showed some composure tonight."

Coach Herb Brooks concurred with Leetch's initial comment: "We talked about the importance of the first five minutes, but we just didn't handle it. We were under siege."

Brooks called a timeout, but this stall had no effect on a wild and highway-fast Russian team. They came at the Americans wave after wave, got to every loose puck in the building. Richter made some nice saves, but the Russians were just a little off target and couldn't score. The USA got its legs, and the up and down game that evolved was the

fastest one could possibly imagine. On one power play, the Russians hit two posts, narrowly missed the net on a couple of other shots, and had the puck in American zone the whole two minutes. At one point, they felt they had scored or that at least the shot was close enough as to require video review. Referee Bill McCreary refused to go to the phone, and after the game the Russians remained incensed that such a close call did not merit further scrutiny.

Time wound down but the pace remained relentless. The USA had its share of chances—notably a Brian Leetch shot that drifted off Khabibulin's glove and the crossbar before skittering into the corner— but the Bulin Wall lived up to his name and gave his team a chance to tie. In the end, with the Wall on the bench, madness ensued in the American end but the Russians could not score.

"When you win a game like this, you still feel like a kid out there," Phil Housley said afterward.

Before, during, and after the handshakes, Russians screamed obscenities at referee McCreary. Danny Markov grabbed his crotch in disgust, Boris Mironov taunted him with mocking signs of thumbs up and shouts of "nice job!" and Darius Kasparaitis spoke in purple prose. Markov received a gross misconduct and one-game suspension for his outburst.

So now the table was set for Canada-USA, Part II: The Men. The all North American, all hockey finals took centre stage to close out these XIX Olympic Winter Games. "It's going to be a great game," Brooks enthused. ✦

BRONZE MEDAL GAME

February 23   **Men**
RUSSIA 7   **BELARUS 2**
12:15 p.m.   **E-Center**

Russia's victory over Belarus provided the expected result. But one player in this game achieved something special. Russian defenseman Igor Kravchuk became the second-ranking Olympic hockey medal winner of all time behind the legendary Vladislav Tretiak. Named to the team as a late replacement for the injured Dmitry Yushkevich, the 35-year-old NHL and Soviet League veteran became the owner of two golds (1988, 1992), a silver (1998), and now a bronze (2002). "Believe me, I haven't been trying to keep score of how many medals I've gotten," said Kravchuk. "I just wanted to play and represent my country." This was likely the final Olympic contest for 41-year-old center Igor Larionov, who won gold medals with the Soviet Union in 1984 and 1988. He made an impressive exit by picking up three assists in the win. "I had a great experience here, and I was really delighted by the way Slava [Fetisov] invited me to play for the national team," said Larionov. "He created a great atmosphere for the players and treated the players in the right way. I'm confident for the future of Russian hockey. It's really bright, and guys like Slava and the people around him can make the future even brighter." Russia became the only nation to win medals in men's hockey in both 1998 and 2002. Belarus was happy to have secured both fourth place in the tournament and the admiration of the world hockey community. "I think now it will be harder for us," said Belarus captain Aleksandr Andrievsky. "[Other teams] will be playing us as hard as we played Sweden." In contrast with the tumult after the semifinals matchup with the USA, this day provided a peaceful ending for Russia and Belarus.   ❖

(above) Playing in his last Olympics, Russia's Igor Larionov stands in the slot looking for a rebound. (right) The Russians had to content themselves with bronze medals at Salt Lake.

(above) The "Russian Rocket," Pavel Bure, performs a small feat of magic on Belarus goalie Sergei Shabanov during Russia's comfortable 7-3 bronze medal win.

WAYNE GRETZKY PREVIEWS CANADA – USA FINALS

"I think the fans are in for a treat." Wayne Gretzky—February 23, 2002.

As Canada prepares for its most important game since game three of the 1996 World Cup, emotion is the key word. "You'll see guys like Yzerman, Mario, Sakic play their top game. They're the players who look forward to this kind of game, who dreamed about it as kids. You'll see them look forward to the challenge," Wayne Gretzky said this afternoon.

Indeed, this Canada-USA finals might be the most-watched hockey game in United States history." Our guys were rooting for the U.S. yesterday," Gretzky admitted. "It's the best thing to happen to the NHL in a while, and it's great for hockey fans in North America."

This is the game in the big picture, a game played before a worldwide audience that even the Stanley Cup finals can't match for global importance. But for coach Pat Quinn, those are ancillary concerns. Far more significant are the teams, their tendencies, their strengths, their weaknesses. "They have an impressive defence and a wonderful counterattack," he summed up.

Indeed, the United States had been the highest-scoring team in the tournament with 24 goals in just five games. But the Americans also had Mike Richter in goal: "I had the distaste of watching him play in game seven in '94 [when Quinn's Vancouver Canucks lost to the Rangers], so we know how he can play," said Quinn.

Gretzky gives full credit to the opponents, even though, of course, he knows what he's after. "There's no question the U.S. has been the best team in the tournament. They have a lot of talent. But nobody remembers who finishes second."

Quinn believes that Canada's strengths lie in its ever-improving play and experience. Between them, Canadian players have won 20 Stanley Cups and played a total of 247 NHL years. Nonetheless, "we have to give them their best game," in order to win, he acknowledged. This means short shifts, no penalties, solid defence. It also means great goaltending and playing "tactically strong. We have to be disciplined, pressure their defence, and go to the net," Quinn noted.

If Canadians want to pump themselves up for the game by using history — as the Americans have throughout this tournament — they need look no further than their track record against the United States at the Olympics. The two nations have played 14 times, and Canada has lost but twice. "It's going to be a great hockey game," Gretzky said with a smile. ❦

GOLD MEDAL GAME

CANADA 5
USA 2

February 24	Men
1:00 p.m.	E-Center

Wayne Gretzky wasn't dressed, but he was on the bench again for the warm-up, his good luck ritual that had been 100 per cent successful for Canada. Mario Lemieux broke his non-ritual by finally shaking hands with the referee and linesmen in the moments leading up to the opening faceoff. Canada wore

"It's (gold medal) going to be remembered for a long time. I've got to imagine the whole country was watching. It's a proud moment for everyone."
STEVE YZERMAN

its good luck white sweaters, the USA their good luck blue. The fans howled chants of "Go Canada Go!" and "USA!" in equal volume. A worldwide audience watched the best two hockey teams at Salt Lake play for a gold medal.

The last game of the Olympics began with intense pressure by Canada, superb puck possession in the American end, and a couple of fine chances to score. But Scott Niedermayer didn't do what coach Quinn had asked his men to do—stay out of the penalty box. His minor slowed down the Canadian attack, and a few minutes later an Owen Nolan error at the USA blueline created a two-on-one and Tony Amonte scored between Martin Brodeur's legs. Advantage America.

The goal did nothing to dissuade an exper-

GAME SUMMARY

First Period
1	USA, Amonte (Weight, Poti)	8:49
2	Canada, Kariya (Pronger, Lemieux)	14:50
3	Canada, Iginla (Sakic, Gagne)	18:33
penalties: Niedermayer (Can)		3:03
Fleury (Can)		10:03

Second Period
4	USA, Rafalski (Modano, Hull)	15:30
5	Canada, Sakic (Jovanovski, Blake)	18:19
penalties: Hull (USA)		9:27
Miller (USA)		10:19
MacInnis (Can)		14:40
Roenick (USA)		16:30

Third Period
6	Canada, Iginla (Yzerman, Sakic)	16:01
7	Canada, Sakic (Iginla)	18:40
penalties: Yzerman (Can)		13:43

In Goal
USA	Mike Richter
CANADA	Martin Brodeur

Shots on Goal
USA	10	14	9	33
CANADA	11	17	11	39

Referee	Bill McCreary
Linesmen	Mike Cvik/Antti Hamalainen

"We were holding them off in the third period, and they made some great plays on the power play. But when we got the fourth goal, it was a big moment, and we could see the end of the tunnel. We're excited. We felt all along the expectations of all the people in Canada. I'll always remember this. It's always fun to be part of a great team. I've been lucky in the NHL to be with a great organization and win two Stanley Cups, and now this."
MARTIN BRODEUR

MAKING HOCKEY HISTORY

ienced Canadian team and wave after wave rolled into the American zone. Chris Pronger saw Lemieux in front of the net as he pinched at the blueline and drilled a pass to the captain. Mario made a play of genius though he never touched the puck. He let the puck slide through his legs while two defencemen and Richter went to him, leaving Paul Kariya in behind with half the net to shoot into (see photo below, top right). Tie game.

A tie was not enough. Canada kept coming and coming, and Joe Sakic

(clockwise) Mario Lemieux looks for a pass at his own blueline; Lemieux' miraculous fake put Paul Kariya in perfect position to tie the score with an open net shot; Jarome Iginla charges to the net to redirect Joe Sakic's pass to give Canada a 2-1 lead.

Canada's Steve Yzerman is stopped in close by Mike Richter on this play, but moments later he and linemate Joe Sakic mob Jarome Iginla after his goal to make it 4-2 late in the third period.

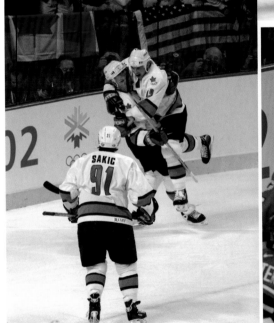

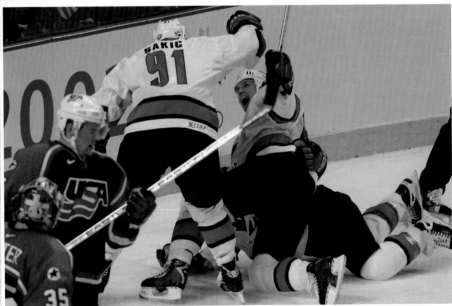

flew down the left wing with Iginla pouring to the net while a blue shirt hung to him. Sakic made a bullet pass nonetheless, and Iginla got his stick down for that millisecond needed to shove the puck past the outstretched leg of Richter (photo p.82, bottom right). In a remarkable period of speed and transition, Canada came out on top 2-1 despite spending four minutes in the penalty box.

belief.

As usual, a successful kill lifts the team that has been short-handed, and when the Americans got a power play of their own a few minutes later, they tied the game. A point shot from Brian Rafalski hit Chris Pronger's stick and snuck between Brodeur's pads. Under five minutes to go, and a 2-2 tie.

Canada came right back with its own man advantage again, however, and this time Joe Sakic ben-

The second period saw two tremendous shifts in emotion and strength. Canada played superior hockey for the first half of the period, forechecking the Americans into the ice and creating turnovers and excellent scoring chances. The resulting surge created a five-on-three power play when Brett Hull and

Aaron Miller took penalties just 52 seconds apart, and Canada had numerous chances to go up by two goals. The highlight of this power play came when Mario Lemieux had an open net and a bouncing puck at his feet, only to have the puck hit the post and bobble into the corner as he lifted his palm upward in dis-

efited from a fortuitous deflection. His wrist shot from the top of the circle hit a stick in front and bounced between Richter, and as the two teams exchanged fluky goals Canada headed to the dressing room up 3-2 with just 20 minutes to go to a gold medal.

While the first two periods were played at a ferocious tempo, Canada slowed the start of the third down to a grinding game of 'sit on the lead

and kill the clock.' And, they were masterful at it. They were on their men before an American knew what to do with the puck, and their stifling play between the bluelines led to good scoring chances or at least the chance to dump the puck in and change lines. Shifts were 20 to 30 seconds, and the American attack that had led the tournament in goals could barely manage to get the puck into the Canadian end let alone maintain sustained possession or pressure.

The endgame came when Jarome Iginla broke in alone to beat Richter and put Canada up by two. The sense of relief on the Canadian bench and in the first row of the upper bowl where Gretzky, Nicholson, Lowe et al sat was palpable, and then when Joe Sakic drilled a perfect wrist shot far side to make it 5-2 at 18:40, the gold medal belonged to Canada. As the clock wound down (or, up, this being international hockey), fans offered a karaoke-quality rendition of 'O, Canada,' and players enjoyed the final seconds from the bench with relief as much as joy. They had won gold, and in doing so they had overcome their fears. ❧

Martin Brodeur takes a look at his gold medal. His father, Denis, won bronze in Cortina in 1956, making them the only father-son medalists in Canadian Olympic hockey history.

Michael Peca
enjoys the
gold medals
presentation
with his
young son.

CANADIAN GOLD 2002

— **86** —

"There's a lot of people singing and dancing in Canada. This is what they've waited for, for a long time. I'm happy for them."
JEREMY ROENICK

"We took a lot of inspiration from how Canada's women's team played against the U.S."
CHRIS PRONGER

"We're a hockey power in the world. Winning the gold kind of reassures Canada."
MARTIN BRODEUR

"I don't think you'll see any country ever dominate international hockey again because everybody's so balanced. It's now down to who gets it together. Look at Sweden — they were awesome. The U.S. just keeps getting better. We're all too balanced now for any team to dominate. I just hope they keep using NHL players in the Olympics."
STEVE YZERMAN

"They won it as a team, but sometimes, it takes one individual. Joe Sakic really stepped up. There are guys on both teams that know what it takes to win, and he had a heck of a game, right from the start. He made a great play on Iginla's goal at the slot on a three-on-two, and when you're a goal scorer the puck seems to find its way to the net. That's what it did for Joe. He's a great player, a great leader. I tip my hat to him and his teammates."
MIKE RICHTER

Captain Mario Lemieux acknowledges the cheers and soaks in the gold-medal atmosphere after the medal presentations, waving his flowers and parading around the ice with his beautiful new jewellery around his neck.

Theo Fleury proved Wayne Gretzky right for naming him to the team. Fleury played his heart out and was full measure for the victorious Canadians.

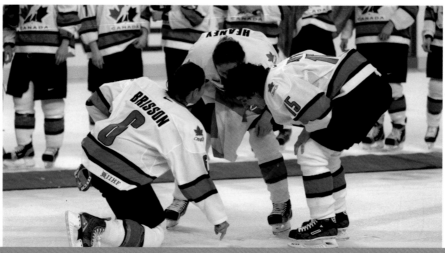

Three members of Canada's women's team point to the spot where the famous "Canadian loonie" was buried at centre ice, much to the anxiety of men's executive director Wayne Gretzky who feared the women might give away their country's secret. Not to worry. The loonie remained where it was until after the men won.

THE GOLDEN LOONIE

Because the Edmonton Oilers' ice at the Skyreach Centre is by far the best sheet in the NHL, the league hired Dan Craig — dubbed 'the Iceman' — and his crew to solve ice problems around North America. This, in turn, led to a gig making and maintaining the ice at the E-Center during the Olympics, and this, in turn, leads to the story of Trent Evans, an Edmonton kind of guy who works under Craig and wears a maple leaf on his sleeve.

While the ice was being put in by Craig's team, Evans thought it would be a cool idea to put a loonie in centre ice. Literally. He started out with a dime, but the next day returned to put a dollar coin over it. He told the players on the men's and wo-

men's team, and they all kept it a secret — until the teams won gold. In fact, after winning their gold on the Thursday, some of the women kissed the ice, alarming men's GM Wayne Gretzky who wanted to ensure its good fortune for the men before anyone found out about the charm.

It did work. After the men won and the crowd had gone home, Gretzky and his assistant, Kevin

Lowe, went out to centre ice to carve the loonie out of its small ice home. "We're going to present it to the Hall of Fame," he said. Sure enough, just a few minutes later, he slipped it into the hand of Phil Pritchard, the Hall's curator (lower photo). "Don't use it in a pop machine," Gretzky said with a smile as he handed it over.

"If I had anything to do with the good luck of both teams winning the gold, I think that's awesome. I'll cherish that forever," Evans said. And so will the men and women players who used the good luck charm to inspire them to whatever greater or lesser degree that may have been!

And the dime? "I still have it at home," he said with a gold-medal grin. ❧

ED BELFOUR
Goaltender—catches left
5'11" 195 lbs.
b. Carman, Manitoba,
April 21, 1965

Ed Belfour was Team Canada's third goalie at the Salt Lake City Olympics behind Martin Brodeur and Curtis Joseph. He was told prior to the Games by executive director Wayne Gretzky and head coach Pat Quinn that he was not likely to see any playing time in the Olympic tournament unless injuries became a factor. Belfour, like all the others given the honour of playing for Canada, was happy to contribute and be part of the team in any way possible. Because each club at the Olympics could dress only two goalies per game, Belfour dressed as backup to Martin Brodeur in the team's third game, a 3-3 tie with the Czechs.

Belfour had previously represented Canada in international competition, playing in 1989-90 with the national team. The following year, he was selected to Team Canada as the club's backup goalie to starter Bill Ranford for the 1991 Canada Cup. Canada went on to win that tournament, which Belfour listed as his most memorable moment in international play until winning Olympic gold in Salt Lake City.

Belfour's nickname is "the Eagle," a name he acquired after he asked an artist to paint a mean-looking bird on his first professional mask back in 1987. The designer wound up using a menacing eagle, and the name stuck. Although he first signed with the Blackhawks in 1987, he was still considered a rookie in 1990-91. That year, he led the NHL with 74 games played and 43 victories and joined Tony Esposito, Frank Brimsek, and Tom Barrasso as the only goaltenders to be awarded the Vezina Trophy as the league's best goalie and the Calder Trophy for rookie of the year in the same season.

As a kid growing up in Manitoba, Belfour's favourite team was the Blackhawks, specifically Stan Mikita and Tony Esposito. While a member of the Blackhawks in the 1990s, Belfour was taught by Russian goaltending legend Vladislav Tretiak, who was signed by the team to instruct their young goaltenders. Czech goalie Dominik Hasek, the backup to Belfour in Chicago, was also tutored by the Hall of Fame Russian netminder. As a tribute to Tretiak, Belfour wears number 20 with the Dallas Stars, the club he led to Stanley Cup glory in 1999. Ironically, Belfour had to go head-to-head against Hasek in the finals.

ROB BLAKE
Defense—shoots right
6'4" 225 lbs.
b. Simcoe, Ontario,
December 19, 1969

Since joining the NHL's Los Angeles Kings in 1990 after a stellar four-year collegiate career at Bowling Green in the NCAA, Rob Blake has consistently been one of the league's top defencemen. On the international stage, Blake has represented Canada on eight occasions, including the 2002 Olympic Winter Games in Salt Lake City, Utah, where he was one of the team's dominant blueliners. He scored the first goal in the game against Sweden on a blistering slap shot, giving Canada a 1-0 lead in what turned out to be a shocking 5-2 loss. Many critics compared that loss with Canada's famous 7-3 defeat in the opening game of the 1972 Summit Series in Montreal against the Soviet Union, when Canada started fast with a 2-0 lead before losing. The fact that the 2002 team rebounded to take gold leads even greater credence to the comparison.

Blake continued his steady play throughout the Salt Lake City Olympics, proving to be Canada's best all-round defenceman. He finished the six-game tournament with a goal and two assists.

The first time Blake represented his country was at the 1991 World Championships in Finland, where Canada came home with the silver medal. He followed that up with a gold medal at the 1994 World Championships, the first time since 1961 that Canada accomplished the feat. He was also a member of the 1997 gold medal championship team and won a silver in 1996. On the 1997 squad, he scored two goals and four points. The biggest disappointment for Blake was coming home from the 1998 Olympics in Nagano without a medal after the heartbreaking overtime shootout loss to the Czech Republic in the semi-finals. If there was a bittersweet moment for Blake, it was being named the top defenceman at the 1998 Olympic competition.

After more than ten seasons with the Los Angeles Kings, Blake was traded to Colorado in time for the Stanley Cup playoff run in the spring of 2001. In 23 playoff games, he scored six goals and 19 points and was a key element in the Avalanche taking its second Stanley Cup in five years, beating the defending champion New Jersey Devils in the finals. He was able to defeat his childhood idol Larry Robinson, who was the coach of the Devils. Following that emotional victory, Blake took the Stanley Cup to his home of Simcoe, population 15,000, in southwestern Ontario. ❧

ERIC BREWER
Defense—shoots left
6'3" 220 lbs.
b. Vernon, British Columbia,
April 17, 1979

Eric Brewer's dreams of becoming a hockey star began at a very young age. Back in his hometown of Vernon, B.C., he often played road hockey with friends in the neighbourhood. Without a doubt, the biggest influence on his development as a player was his father, Frank, who coached him for eight years of youth hockey.

Although he has now represented Canada internationally on three occasions, Brewer's inclusion on the 2002 Canadian Olympic Team in Salt Lake City clearly indicated that he his now regarded as one of the premier defensemen in the world. He got his first taste of

international action as an 18-year-old at the 1998 World Junior Hockey Championships, where he was one of the team's assistant captains.

The selection to the 2002 Canadian Olympic Team is by far the biggest accomplishment in the young hockey career of Brewer, a rising star with the NHL's Edmonton Oilers. Although he was used primarily as Canada's seventh defenceman, the coaching staff was confident enough

to use him at key points in the Olympic tournament, giving workhorses like Rob Blake, Chris Pronger, and Scott Niedermayer a chance to catch their breath.

Brewer played three years of major junior hockey with Prince George in the Western Hockey League before joining the New York Islanders for the 1998-99 season. He was traded to his current team, the Oilers, on June 24, 2000 for another Olympian, Czech Roman Hamrlik, who gained much unwanted notoriety for a crosscheck to the back of Canada's Theo Fleury during a 3-3 tie in round-robin play in Salt Lake. ♦

For many years Martin Brodeur has been acknowledged as one of the world's greatest goaltenders. In 1995, he led the New Jersey Devils to their first-ever Stanley Cup championship and followed that up with a second Cup victory in 2000. Despite being considered one of the best at his craft, Brodeur had dressed in just five international games for Canada prior to Salt Lake. In 1996, he played in three games on the silver medal winning team at the World Championships and later that year appeared in two World Cup games as the Canadians once again took silver behind a strong United States team.

In 1998, Brodeur was selected to the Canadian Olympic Team that played in Nagano, but he did not play because starter Patrick Roy of the Colorado Avalanche played every game. Although Bro-deur did not see any action, failing to win a medal in Nagano was certainly one of the biggest disappointments of his international career. At the start of the Salt Lake Olympics, it appeared Brodeur would once again be left looking on from the outside when Team Canada coach Pat Quinn announced that Curtis Joseph would be the team's starting netminder.

Brodeur was told he would play the second game against Germany. Only after that would team officials determine who to start for the all-important third game based on the results of games one and two. Joseph was uncharacteristically shaky in a 5-2 loss to Sweden and Brodeur was steady, if unspecta-

MARTIN BRODEUR
Goaltender—catches left
6'2" 205 lbs.
b. Montreal, Quebec,
May 6, 1972

cular, in a 3-2 win over Germany. It was certainly good enough to earn him the nod against the defending gold medallists from the Czech Republic. That 3-3 tie ensured that Brodeur would be the team's goalie going into the medal round. He led Canada to wins over Finland and

Belarus before facing the Americans in the gold medal game.

As do true champions, Brodeur saved his best performance for the final. The key moment in the game may well have come early in the third period. With Canada leading 3-2, Brodeur kicked out his right pad to stop a one-timer from Brett Hull. "That was the turning point in the game," said Wayne Gretzky. "Soon after that we went down the ice and scored to make it 4-2." In five Olympic games, Brodeur allowed just nine goals.

There is Olympic history within the Brodeur family. Martin's father, Denis, was the starter for Canada's bronze medal-winning team at the 1956 Olympics in Cortina. The elder Brodeur later became the official photographer for the Montreal Canadiens and captured the most famous goal in hockey history at the Luzhniki Sports Palace in Moscow when Paul Henderson scored the series-winning goal against the Soviet Union in 1972.

Brodeur has been a workhorse in goal for the Devils, appearing in at least 70 games in five of the past six NHL seasons. He has been voted to the starting lineup in the NHL All-Star Game in 1996 and 1999. Brodeur and his Team Canada goaltending teammate, Ed Belfour, share a rare honour with a third Olympic goalie, USA's Tom Barrasso, as being the only three goalies in the past 20 years to have won the Calder Trophy, signifying the NHL's top rookie. Brodeur won the award in 1994, Belfour in 1991, and Barrasso back in 1984. ❧

THEOREN FLEURY
Right Wing—shoots right
5'6" 180 lbs.
b. Oxbow, Saskatchewan,
June 29, 1968

Fleury is the smallest player in the NHL, but his supporters say he has the biggest heart when it comes to competitive fire and desire. His unparalleled work ethic and leadership qualities have long impressed Canadian hockey executives, most notably Wayne Gretzky, who have never wavered from selecting the 5'6" dynamo to represent Canada on numerous occasions. At the conclusion of the 2002 Olympics, Fleury was emotional in thanking all those who had stood behind him.

From the drop of the first puck in Salt Lake, Fleury proved he was ready to help Canada bring back the gold. His best game of the tournament was likely in the 3-3 tie against the Czech Republic, where he consistently drove goaltender Dominik Hasek to distraction. Near the end of the game, Fleury was the victim of a crosscheck to the back just outside the Czech crease at the hand and stick of Czech defender Roman Hamrlik. The hit drew a tremendous amount of media publicity and was the driving force behind Canadian executive Wayne Gretzky's now famous post-game tirade in support of his team.

Fleury's first memories of playing hockey date back to when he was five years old, donning skates in his hometown of Binscarth, Manitoba. Watching hockey as a kid, his favour-

ite team was the New York Islanders, but his individual favourite player was Hall of Famer Denis Savard, primarily because of his size, or lack thereof.

As a junior, Fleury was a scoring star with Moose Jaw of the Western Hockey League for four years and was twice named to the Canadian Junior National Team that competed at the World Junior Hockey Championships. His only previous international experience came while playing for Canada in the Under-17 tournament in 1994-95. In 1987, the Canadian Juniors came home without gold after a Soviet-instigated brawl disqualified them. Under Fleury's leadership, that team regrouped the following year, taking gold. Fleury provided much of the offensive spark for the club, scoring

six goals and eight points in just six games. He was rewarded for his strong play by being named to the tournament All-Star Team, along with other 2002 Olympians Teppo Numminen of Finland and Sergei Fedorov of Russia. Current 2002 Olympics teammate Joe Sakic was also on that 1988 gold medal winning junior squad.

Two years later, as a member of the NHL's Calgary Flames, Fleury was again representing his country, this time at the World Hockey Championships, where he scored eleven points in nine games. Despite his strong individual performance, Canada came up short when the medals were handed out. In 1991, Fleury returned with his Canadian mates where they claimed silver at the Worlds. In the fall of 1991, he was selected to Team Canada, which won the Canada Cup.

The next opportunity for Fleury to represent Canada came in 1996, at the first World Cup. In eight games, Fleury contributed six points, but the Canadians faced Mike Richter, who was nothing short of spectacular in stealing victory for the Americans in the championship finals. However, the biggest disappointment of Fleury's international career came at the 1998 Nagano Olympics, where Team Canada failed to win a medal. ❧

Big, rugged Adam Foote was definitely in the original plans for Team Canada at the 2002 Salt Lake City Olympics. The only concern was his health. Foote missed the first 16 games of the 2001-02 season following an off-season surgery on his right shoulder. It's no coincidence that his club team, Colorado, started playing better when he returned, and in the months leading up to the Olympics he proved that he was, indeed, healthy and ready to play.

In Salt Lake, Foote consistently aided the Canadian cause by blocking shots and playing physically and reliably in his own end. Offensively, he contributed a goal. He was especially strong in the 3-3 tie with the Czech Republic and in the 5-2 gold medal win over United States.

Foote grew up in Toronto and played his major junior hockey with the Sault Ste Marie Greyhounds of the OHL. He was a member of the

ADAM FOOTE
Defense—shoots right
6'2" 215 lbs.
b. Toronto, Ontario,
July 10, 1971

1991 Ontario championship team that played in the Memorial Cup in Quebec, which was eventually won by the Spokane Chiefs of the WHL.

Upon making the transition to the NHL, Foote played just six games in the minors before being called up to the Quebec Nordiques. After four years in Quebec, Foote and the organization moved to Colorado and

were renamed the Avalanche. In its first year in Denver, the Avalanche won the Stanley Cup. Despite being one of the NHL's elite teams over the next four years, the Avalanche failed to reach the Cup finals again until the 2000-01 season, when they defeated the defending champion New Jersey Devils in a thrilling seven-game series.

Foote gained his first international exposure playing for the Canadian National Team for three games in 1989-90 at the age of 18. Coming off the 1996 Stanley Cup championship that spring, he was chosen by Glen Sather to participate in the World Cup that September. Foote was a solid performer for Canada in his eight games, which ended in a tough loss against the USA in the finals. Even more amazing was the fact that Foote played the last few games with a cracked bone in his foot.

SIMON GAGNE
Left Wing—shoots left
6' 180 lbs.
b. Ste. Foy, Quebec,
February 29, 1980

Speedy left winger Simon Gagne of the Philadelphia Flyers was considered by many to be one of the key ingredients to Canadian success at the 2002 Olympics. On the big ice surface, players such as Gagne, Paul Kariya, and Joe Sakic were able to showcase their offensive skills.

Gagne was the Flyers' first choice, 22nd overall, in the 1998 NHL Entry Draft from the QMJHL's Quebec Remparts. When told he was selected to Team Canada's Olympic roster, Gagne responded "I can't believe it. To be so young and have a chance to play with the best players in the world. A couple of years ago I made the Flyers as a 19-year-old, and that was hard to believe. But I never expected this." At tour-nament's end, Gagne was still five days shy of his 22nd birthday.

Throughout the Salt Lake Olympics, Gagne's free-wheeling style of play set up many offensive scoring chances for Canada. He finished the six-game tournament with a goal and three assists, including one helper on Jarome Iginla's first of two goals in the 5-2 gold medal-winning game against the United States.

Prior to Salt Lake, Gagne's only other international experience came in 1999 as a member of the silver medal Canadian National Junior Team where he scored seven goals and eight points in seven games. He was named to the NHL's All-Rookie Team in 2000 with Philadelphia, scoring 20 goals and 48 points in 80 games.

Gagne remembers going to Le Colisee in Quebec to watch the Nordiques play against Mario Lemieux and the Pittsburgh Penguins. Ten years later, he realized a dream when he played on a line with Lemieux for the North American All-Stars at the 2001 NHL All-Star Game in Denver. And now, gold with Mario in Salt Lake!

JAROME IGINLA
Right Wing—shoots right
6'1" 200 lbs.
b. Edmonton, Alberta,
July 1, 1977

Heading into the 2002 Salt Lake Olympics, Jarome Iginla of the Calgary Flames was the hottest player in the NHL, leading the league in scoring. Canada GM and executive director Wayne Gretzky felt that the combination of Iginla's strong offensive season, fast skating, and previous success at the international level would make him a great fit for the team. However, entering the NHL season, he was considered a longshot to make it. In fact, he was a last-minute invitee to the Canadian Olympic training camp in September 2001.

Iginla saved his best for last at Salt Lake City. In the thrilling gold medal game against the United States, he scored twice and set up numerous other scoring chances in a 5-2 win,

marking the first time Canada had taken gold at the Olympics since 1952 in Oslo, Norway. His final statistics from Salt Lake consisted of three goals and an assist.

Iginla achieved success in hockey at a young age and was a member of the two-time Memorial Cup champion Kamloops Blazers in 1994 and 1995. Growing up in Edmonton, he always admired the Oilers.

Gretzky, Fuhr, and Messier were his idols because, as Iginla plainly puts it, "they were the best players on the best team in the NHL."

Surprisingly, Iginla played primarily in goal until the age of nine, when he decided he wanted to try a skating position. Immediately, he realized he had a knack for scoring. He first represented Canada in an Under-18 tournament and later won gold at the 1996 World Junior Hockey Championships in Boston. It was a great offensive performance for Iginla. He scored five goals and 12 points in six games and was selected to the All-Star Team. He was also named the tournament's top forward. A year later, he helped Canada win a gold medal at the World Championships in 1997. ❧

CURTIS JOSEPH
Goaltender—catches left
5'11" 190 lbs.
b. Keswick, Ontario,
April 29, 1967

For many years Curtis Joseph has been one of Canada's premier goaltenders, starring for the St. Louis Blues, Edmonton Oilers, and now the Toronto Maple Leafs. Despite being near the top, he often found himself in the shadows of the likes of Patrick Roy when it came to international competition, including the 1998 Olympic Winter Games in Nagano. When Roy announced he would not play for Canada in 2002, Joseph was quietly installed as the number-one goaltender heading into the games at Salt Lake. The job was his to lose. Martin Brodeur was to start game two against Germany, but if Joseph played well in the opener against Sweden, it was widely speculated that he would be given the job for the rest of the Olympic tournament.

The entire Canadian team came out flat in the contest against Sweden, including Joseph, losing 5-2. Brodeur then played well enough against Germany to warrant the start against the Czechs, and he cemented his status as the number-one netminder follow-

ing a solid performance in a 3-3 tie. Joseph was relegated to the role of backup for the remainder of the tournament, but harboured no ill will.

Despite many years of NHL success, "CUJO" did not represent Canada internationally until 1996 when he helped Canada win the silver medal at the World Championships just a few months short of his 29th birthday. He was also Canada's starting goalie for the team that finished runner-up at the World Cup in the fall of 1996.

Joseph was a late bloomer in hockey. At 17, he was still playing Junior B with the King City Dukes in 1984-85 and then played two seasons of Provincial Junior A with Richmond Hill. At the age of 21, he guided Notre Dame school in Saskatchewan to the

Centennial Cup title in 1988. He was not drafted by any NHL team, so he enrolled at the University of Wisconsin, winning numerous awards while going 21-11-5 in 38 games. The St. Louis Blues signed him to a free agent contract on June 16, 1989.

"CUJO" realized his lifelong dream to play for the Toronto Maple Leafs when he signed a free agent deal on July 15, 1998. In his first season, the team set a club record with 35 wins in 1998-99 and he did not lose more than two games in a row all year. In 1999-2000, "CUJO" broke his own record by posting 36 wins and finished third in Vezina Trophy voting behind 2002 Olympians Olaf Kolzig of Germany, playing for the Washington Capitals, and Czech Roman Turek of the St. Louis Blues.

Joseph's now famous nickname "CUJO" is derived from the first two letters of his first and last name and also a Steven King novel of the same name. It was given to him by Robert Dirk, a former teammate in St. Louis in the early 1990s.

ED JOVANOVSKI
Defense—shoots left
6'2" 210 lbs.
b. Windsor, Ontario,
June 26, 1976

Defenseman Ed Jovanovski of the Vancouver Canucks was a late starter to hockey, not picking up the game until the age of eleven. Prior to hockey his sport of choice was always soccer because his father played at the semi-pro level in Europe. "It was more or less just wanting to follow in father's footsteps," he says. However, when he got a taste of the ice, he knew there was no going back. "Once I got the skates on, I just tossed soccer aside."

In Salt Lake City, Jovanovski excelled on the large ice surface, displaying a speed that many observers did not realize he had. The consensus was that he, along with Rob Blake, were the two biggest contributors to the Canadian defence. Team Canada assistant coach Ken Hitchcock said, "If you're coaching a hockey club, you want a guy like Jovanovski because he is such a great personality. He has that carefree recklessness on the ice. I think he's an emotional, great player." Having the opportunity to play in the Olympics was definitely a dream come true. "Other than getting married and having kids, this is one of the best things in my life. I called home and my parents were in tears

when I told them I made the team. They became Canadian citizens 25 years ago."

Heading into the gold medal game against the U.S., Jovanovski was a key contributor in each of Canada's five games, assisting on two goals. He then set up Joe Sakic for what proved to be the gold medal-winning goal on the power-play late in the second period against the Americans in a 5-2 victory.

Jovanovski's talents first became apparent when he scored 25 goals and 65 points in 50 games with the OMHA's Windsor Bulldogs at the age of 15 in 1991-92. After a year of Junior B hockey, he had two excel-

lent seasons with the Windsor Spitfires of the OHL. He scored 23 goals and 65 points and was deemed the toughest defenceman in the league to play against. He also was not afraid to play it tough as well, collecting 198 minutes in penalties. This all-round completeness in his game saw him selected as the first overall pick by the Florida Panthers in the 1994 NHL Entry Draft. Jovanovski got his first international experience back in 1995 as a key member of the gold medal Canadian club at the World Junior Championships, held in Red Deer, Alberta. Olympic teammate and close friend Ryan Smyth was also on that winning squad.

In his rookie season in the NHL, Jovanovski helped the Panthers to an improbable run to the Stanley Cup finals where they were beaten by the Colorado Avalanche. His excellent rookie season and playoffs ensured him an invitation to Canada's silver medal-winning team at the 1996 World Cup of Hockey, although he was an alternate and did not actually play. He has also answered the call to play for his country at the 1998 and 2000 World Championships. ♦

PAUL KARIYA
Left Wing—shoots left
5'10" 175 lbs.
b. Vancouver, British Columbia,
October 16, 1974

The speedy Paul Kariya loves to play on the international-sized ice surface where a player with his skating ability is allowed to excel. And, he did not disappoint Canadians at the 2002 Olympics in Salt Lake City. Kariya missed the 1998 Olympic Winter Games in Nagano because of post concussion syndrome. However, in 2002, he was one of Canada's top players, turning in especially strong performances in a win over Germany and a tie against the Czech Republic in round-robin action.

The biggest single contribution Kariya made for Canada at Salt Lake was scoring the tying goal in the gold medal game midway through the first period after the United States had taken an early lead. Canada had been dominating, with nothing to show on the scoreboard, until Kariya popped home a beautiful goal thanks to a smart-thinking Mario Lemieux who faked taking a pass from defenseman Chris Pronger. Lemieux let the puck slide between his legs to a waiting Kariya. USA goaltender Mike Richter mo-

mentarily took the bait, thinking Lemieux would shoot, and the slight hesitation was enough to leave him out of position and give Kariya a huge empty net. In six games, Kariya scored three goals and four points.

Kariya, selected fourth overall in the 1993 NHL Entry Draft by the Anaheim Mighty Ducks, played his junior hockey in Penticton of the BCJHL before enrolling at the University of Maine, where he won the Hobey Baker Award as the top player in the NCAA in 1993. He returned to play another season of collegiate hockey but left the team

after playing just 12 games so that he might join the Canadian National Team. In 23 games, he scored seven goals and 41 points. He joined the NHL and the Mighty Ducks in the lockout-shortened season of '94-'95, where he had 18 goals and 39 points in 47 games.

Kariya first represented Canada in 1992 at the World Junior Championships. He returned in 1993, helping Canada to win the gold, scoring eight points in seven games. A few months later, he joined the Canadian National Team for the 1993 World Championships, scoring nine points in eight games. He now has two Olympic medals, having been a member of the 1994 silver medal team in Lillehammer, Norway. In that tournament, Kariya registered three goals and seven points in eight games. He also won a gold medal at the 1994 World Championships and a silver medal at the 1996 competition where he was named the tournament's best forward. Injuries forced him to miss both the 1996 World Cup of Hockey and the 1998 Olympics in Nagano.

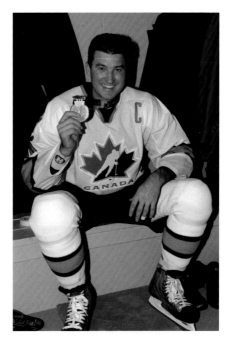

MARIO LEMIEUX
Centre—shoots right
6'4" 225 lbs.
b. Montreal, Quebec,
October 5, 1965

Prior to the gold medal triumph at the 2002 Salt Lake City Olympics, it had been 15 years since Mario Lemieux competed for Canada on an international stage. In September 1987, he scored the second most important goal in Canadian hockey history, taking that famous pass from Wayne Gretzky and scoring the winning goal as Canada defeated the Soviet Union in the third and deciding game of the Canada Cup at Hamilton's Copps Coliseum. Only Paul Henderson's 1972 goal against the Soviets ranks higher.

Upon receiving the official news that Lemieux was exchanging his owner's suit and tie with the Pittsburgh Penguins for his old sweater number 66, it didn't take long for Team Canada executives, led by Wayne Gretzky, to announce that Lemieux would not only be selected to the Olympic team, but would also serve as captain. It was evident that he still had the offensive touch, scoring 35 goals and 76 points in just 43 games in a successful 2000-01 return season. But, an entire nation held its collective breath in the fall of 2001 when Lemieux's hip began bothering him and he was forced to sit out many games before and after Christmas. However, a rested Lemieux showed up at Salt Lake ready to perform. "My main goal has been to make it to the Olympics," Lemieux noted before the Games.

Lemieux didn't dress for Canada's 3-2 win over Germany. He played his best game against the Czech Republic, scoring two of Canada's goals in a 3-3 tie against Dominik Hasek and the defending Olympic champions. Coming in to the Salt Lake City Games, Lemieux had scored six goals and assisted on another 12 against Hasek in 18 NHL games, so if anyone could claim to have had good fortune against the star netminder, it would be Mario.

In the championship finals, Lemieux was at his best. He had several glorious scoring opportunities, including an open net shot which somehow rang off the post and out. "I don't think he ever missed one like that in his life," Gretzky laughed after the game. "I just couldn't believe it" a still shocked Lemieux said

of his missed open net following the game. Although he did not score in the final, he was part of a beautiful passing play which led to Canada's tying the game at 1-1. The goal lifted the confidence on the Canadian bench, and from there they continued to take the play to the Americans for much of the game. When it was all over, the scoreboard read 5-2. Lemieux had fulfilled the dream —his own dream, and one that a nation had not realized in 50 years.

Lemieux first performed internationally for Canada as a 17-year-old at the 1983 World Junior Hockey Championships where he was a teammate of fellow 2002 Olympic teammate Steve Yzerman. In seven games, he scored five goals and ten points as Canada brought home the bronze medal. His next appearance on the international stage came in 1985 where he helped Canada to the silver medal at the World Championships, scoring four goals and ten points in nine games. Next up was the 1987 NHL Rendez-vous tournament against the Soviet Union, a replacement that year for the annual All-Star Game. Lemieux's greatest international achievement prior to the Olympic gold was the aforementioned winning goal in the 1987 Canada Cup, where he led the tournament with eleven goals in nine games and was named to the tournament All-Star Team.

Playing in Salt Lake in 2002 marked the third time Eric Lindros had been a Canadian Olympian. When executive director Wayne Gretzky and the Team Canada brass were set to announce the roster for the 2002 Olympics, speculation abounded as to whether Lindros would be selected. Gretzky answered those questions by saying, "If Eric is healthy, he will be part of our team." All seemed well, and Lindros got off to a fast start with the Rangers. But on December 28, 2001, he suffered a mild concussion, the seventh of his career. He was placed on injured reserve for three days before returning.

At the Olympics, Lindros seemed tentative in the first three games and was benched by coach Pat Quinn for the entire third period in the win against Finland. The move clearly caught the attention of Lindros, who returned in fine form for the game against Belarus, and looked like the Lindros of old, crunching players with hard body checks and even contributing a goal in Canada's 7-1 win which allowed them to advance to the gold medal game against the United States. In the championship game, Lindros played on a line with Owen Nolan and Ryan Smyth against the big USA trio of Mike Modano, John LeClair, and Brett Hull.

In 1992, and not yet 19, Lindros helped Canada to the silver medal in Albertville, France. The gold went to the Unified Team after it beat Canada 3-1 in the finals.

By 1998, Lindros had established himself as one of the premier players and leaders in the game. He was selected to captain Team Canada by

ERIC LINDROS
Centre—shoots right
6'4" 240 lbs.
b. London, Ontario,
February 28, 1973

general manager Bobby Clarke of the Philadelphia Flyers, who said it was time for Lindros to "carry the torch for Canada and be a leader in international competitions." Lindros co-led the club in scoring at Nagano, along with Joe Nieuwendyk.

Lindros was a star in junior hockey and helped the OHL's Oshawa Generals to the Memorial Cup championship in 1990. He caused a stir when he refused to sign with the Quebec Nordiques, who drafted him first overall in the 1991 NHL Entry Draft. So determined was he not to play for the Nordiques that Lindros chose to return to junior, but after 13 games back in Oshawa, he joined the Canadian National Team to prepare for the 1992 Olympics.

One year later, Lindros was dealt by the Nordiques to the Philadelphia Flyers in one of the biggest trades in NHL history.

The first time Lindros donned the Maple Leaf sweater for Canada was at the age of 15, when he played two games with the national team in Halifax, Nova Scotia in 1988-89. Despite his age, he was already close to 6'4" and 210 lbs. and was the biggest player on the ice. In 1990 and 1991, he was a key contributor to Canada's back-to-back gold medal victories at the World Junior Championships. In 1991, he was selected to the WJC All-Star Team, along with 2002 Olympians Martin Rucinsky of the Czech Republic and Dmitry Yushkevich of Russia, both of whom were forced to miss the Salt Lake City Games due to injury.

At the age of 18, Lindros earned a spot on Team Canada for the 1991 Canada Cup, making him the only non-NHLer to play. He is perhaps best remembered from that tournament for his thunderous check on Sweden's Ulf Samuelsson, which resulted in a broken collarbone for the big Swedish defender. Canada went on to win the tournament, beating Sweden in the finals. In 1993, Lindros joined Team Canada for the World Championships, but despite leading the tournament in scoring with eleven goals and 17 points and being named the best forward, he was unable to elevate Canada to a medal position. In 1996, Lindros was a member of the Canadian team in the World Cup. In eight games, he contributed three goals and six points. ♣

At 38, Al MacInnis was the elder statesman of Canada's gold medal winning team at the 2002 Salt Lake City Olympics. A veteran of 19 NHL seasons, MacInnis was chosen to the team on the basis of his solid play alongside his St. Louis Blues defense partner, Chris Pronger, and his excellent leadership qualities in the dressing room. After each struggled with different partners in the opening-game loss to Sweden, the two were paired together for the rest of the tournament.

MacInnis and his Olympic teammates realized that a win over Germany was necessary to provide confidence for the team and for the millions of concerned Canadians who had followed the discouraging play in the game against Sweden. Although Canada squeaked out a narrow 3-2 win over the Germans, many players, including MacInnis, showed signs of adapting to the international rules and adjusting to the larger ice surface. By the third game against the Czechs, the Canadians were playing as everyone had expected, outplaying the defending Olympic champions for a good portion of the game and coming away with a well-deserved 3-3 tie.

AL MacINNIS
Defense—shoots right
6'2" 210 lbs.
b. Inverness, Nova Scotia,
July 11, 1963

After going 1-1-1 in round-robin action, Canada faced Finland in the first game of the medal round, turning back the Finns 2-1, and then beating Belarus 7-1. MacInnis nearly scored a goal in the latter game, ringing a sizzling slap shot off the crossbar. When asked if he was trying to intimidate the Belarussian goalie by aiming high, MacInnis replied "I was trying to score. But, he chose to be a goalie." Although MacInnis failed to earn a point in the Olympic competition, he played exceptionally well, especially in the gold medal game.

MacInnis was selected 15th overall in the 1981 NHL Entry Draft by the Calgary Flames from the Kitchener Rangers of the OHL. In 1981, he helped the Rangers to the Memorial Cup finals where they lost to the defending champion Cornwall Royals, led by Hall of Famer Dale Hawerchuk. The following year, the Rangers returned, this time winning the Memorial Cup. MacInnis, Brian Bellows, Scott Stevens, and Jeff Larmer spearheaded the victory.

It was not until 1990, at the age of 27, that MacInnis first represented Canada in international hockey. He played nine games at the World Championships, scoring one goal and four points. In 1991, he was an instrumental force in helping Canada to win the Canada Cup. The team beat the USA in the finals, and MacInnis was named a tournament All-Star. In eight games, he scored two goals and six points. The only other international experience for MacInnis came at the 1998 Nagano Olympics.

MacInnis was a member of the 1989 Stanley Cup champion Calgary Flames, winning the Conn Smythe Trophy as the playoff MVP. ✦

SCOTT NIEDERMAYER
Defense—shoots left
6'1" 200 lbs.
b. Edmonton, Alberta,
August 31, 1973

Scott Niedermayer, selected 3rd overall by the New Jersey Devils in the 1991 NHL Entry Draft from the WHL's Kamloops Blazers, is regarded as one of the top offensive defenceman in the NHL. He was chosen as one of Canada's elite eight selected in the fall of 2001 for the Salt Lake City Games.

When the Team Canada coaching staff huddled together for its meetings on player personnel, the need for an offensive, rushing defenceman came up. It was unanimous that Scott Niedermayer fit the bill perfectly.

Niedermayer's first international experience came at the 1991 World Junior Championships where he and fellow 2002 Olympics teammate Eric Lindros helped guide the team to the gold medal. He returned in 1992, but Canada failed to win a medal, though Niedermayer was selected to the tournament All-Star Team. In the 1996 World Cup, he suited up for all eight Canadian games, scoring a goal and four points.

In Salt Lake City, Niedermayer was effective in clearing his own zone and excelled at passing in the wide lanes of the 100-foot-wide international ice. He had particularly strong showings in the 3-3 tie against the Czechs, the 2-1 win over Finland, and the gold medal-winning 5-2 triumph over the USA. During the six-games, Niedermayer contributed offensively with a goal and an assist, but also played a very responsible defensive game, which helped to limit the opposition's scoring chances.

As a 16-year-old junior with the Kamloops Blazers in 1989-90, Niedermayer's coach was Team Canada's Salt Lake assistant coach Ken Hitchcock. Together, they led the Blazers to the Memorial Cup championship. Niedermayer, having now added Olympic gold to his collection of medals, has the rare distinction of having won the Memorial Cup, a World Junior Championship gold medal, and a Stanley Cup (with the New Jersey Devils in 1995 and 2000).

JOE NIEUWENDYK
Centre—shoots left
6'1" 205 lbs.
b. Oshawa, Ontario,
September 10, 1966

One of the most consistent performers for Canada at the 2002 Olympic Winter Games was Joe Nieuwendyk. The 35-year-old created numerous scoring opportunities throughout the tournament and seemed to be at his best when the most was on the line. During the six-game Olympic tournament, Nieuwendyk contributed a goal and an assist and seemed to enjoy the free-wheeling style of play allowed on the bigger ice surface.

Following the dramatic 5-2 win over the United States to claim the gold medal, Nieuwendyk said triumphantly, "This is for all of Canada. We just couldn't let everyone down." The fortitude and inner strength was something the entire Canadian team managed to accomplish when it mattered most. Throughout the tournament, Nieuwendyk's biggest and most vocal supporter was his brother, Gil, who cheered him on in the stands.

Between games and practices at Salt Lake City, Nieuwendyk liked to relax by taking in the speed-skating,

a favourite event of many players on the hockey team.

Before winning gold in Salt Lake City, Nieuwendyk's most memorable international experience had been the Nagano Olympics in 1998, where he played alongside Wayne Gretzky. He performed well offensively, co-leading the team in scoring with Eric Lindros, at five points apiece.

The first time Nieuwendyk represented Canada was at the World

Junior Championships in Hamilton, Ontario in 1986. "It was an overwhelming feeling to know the whole country was watching," he said. The pressure from the crowd and a nation obviously didn't have much of an adverse effect on the lanky centre. He registered the third-highest point total of the tournament, scoring five goals and 12 points in seven games en route to a silver medal showing. His next international appearance came in 1990 at the World Championships where he played one game.

Nieuwendyk was picked to play for Canada at the 1991 Canada Cup but an injury in training camp prevented him from playing. His next opportunity came seven years later when he was chosen to play in the 1998 Olympics. Nieuwendyk is a Stanley Cup champion in Calgary in 1989 and Dallas in 2000. And now, he's an Olympic gold medallist. During the emotional playing of the Canadian anthem, Nieuwendyk held his young daughter, Tyra, in his arms on the ice.

OWEN NOLAN
Right Wing—shoots right
6'1" 210 lbs.
b. Belfast, Northern Ireland,
February 12, 1972

Owen Nolan was born in Belfast, Northern Ireland but moved to Thorold, Ontario, a small town of 15,000 just west of Niagara Falls, when he was just seven months old.

Chosen as one of the original eight for the Canadian Olympic Team in the fall of 2001, Nolan found himself under increased scrutiny and pressure from the Canadian media because he had a slow start to the 2001-02 season. A nagging shoulder injury and an assortment of minor injuries had dulled his normally feisty game considerably and he was not scoring with the same frequency that saw him reach the 44-goal plateau for the San Jose Sharks in the 1999-2000 season.

Team GM and executive director Wayne Gretzky felt Nolan was the best Canadian on the ice in the disappointing opening loss to Sweden. Nolan responded with a strong second game against Germany, banging and crashing along the boards and using his size to intimidate and create opportunities for the other forwards on his line. His strong play continued in the game against the Czechs, where he set up numerous scoring opportunities. Despite failing to score during the six games of the tournament, Nolan was creating excellent chances in the offensive zone and assisted on three Canadian goals.

As the clock began to count down, with Canada a mere seconds away from their long-awaited gold medal, the players and coaches on the bench could barely contain themselves before leaping onto the ice as the final buzzer sounded, making a mad dash toward goaltender Martin Brodeur. All except Owen Nolan. He was busy capturing the final moments on his personal camera. "I wasn't going on," he explained. "I was too busy filming." He said his motivation was to capture forever the tremendous emotion of winning the Olympic gold.

In his only other appearance representing Canada, Nolan tied for second in team scoring at the 1997 World Championships, scoring four goals and seven points. The outcome produced a gold medal for Canada.

Coming out of junior hockey, Nolan was considered the most complete player in the world. He was chosen first overall in the 1990 NHL Entry Draft by the Quebec Nordiques following a season with the OHL's Cornwall Royals where he recorded 51 goals and 110 points in 58 games. During his rookie NHL season, he led the Nordiques in scoring with 42 goals and topped the 30-goal plateau in four of the next five NHL seasons. He was traded to the San Jose Sharks on October 25, 1995, shortly after the Nordiques moved to Colorado and became the Avalanche. Nolan was named San Jose's captain on October 28, 1998.

It would be hard to argue there is a better all-round defensive forward playing hockey today than Canada's Michael Peca. "He's the best two-way player in the game," says Mark Parrish, Peca's teammate on the New York Islanders. "I can't think of another guy who plays as well defensively and now he's showing he can play offensively."

It seemed obvious to most hockey observers that Peca would be included on Canada's roster at the Salt Lake City Olympics, but Peca was taking nothing for granted even after finding out that he had, indeed, earned a spot. "Playing for your country is a privilege, not a right, and I feel blessed to be in the right place at the right time."

In Salt Lake City, Peca started playing on the wing. After one

MICHAEL PECA

Centre—shoots right
5'11" 190 lbs.
b. Toronto, Ontario,
March 26, 1974

game, coach Pat Quinn moved him to centre and Peca returned to his checking form. In five games with Canada, he was effective in neutralizing the other country's top scorers while managing to help set up two Canadian goals during the course of the Olympic tournament.

Peca first represented Canada at an Under-18 tournament in Japan. He won a gold medal at the World Junior Championships in 1994 and answered the call to play for his country at the 2001 World Championships, where he was named team captain. He suffered a fractured cheekbone in the third game, however, and missed the rest of the tournament.

A tenacious checker, Peca has proven that a player doesn't have to be a giant to dish out bone-crunching bodychecks. Time and time again, the 190-pounder has used his tremendous technique to block opponents with clean, open-ice hits. His great speed and awareness of others on the ice also generates good offensive scoring situations. In 1998-99, as captain of the Buffalo Sabres, Peca scored 27 goals and 56 points in 82 games while leading the Sabres to the Stanley Cup finals.

Team Canada 2002 Olympic officials had to feel secure in knowing their defense would be in good hands heading to Salt Lake City: they had three of the last four Norris Trophy winners in the lineup. Los Angeles' Rob Blake won in 1998, Al MacInnis of the St. Louis Blues in 1999, and MacInnis' defensive partner Chris Pronger, who in 1999-2000 took the rare double in winning the Norris and Hart Trophy as the NHL's most valuable player.

In the game most Canadians would prefer to forget, Pronger and the rest of Team Canada came out on the losing end in its first game against Sweden in Salt Lake City, a 5-2 loss. "We just seemed out of place," Pronger lamented afterward. "We just were not able to properly read how to defend that open style of play on the bigger ice."

Team Canada head coach Pat Quinn opted to tinker with his defensive pairings, but soon realized Pronger worked best when partnered with his St. Louis teammate Al MacInnis. The duo remained a strong unit in the 3-3 tie against the Czechs and improved with each game.

From the onset of the tournament, Canadian hockey commentator Don Cherry expressed his concern for what he believed was a design flaw in the Plexiglas surrounding the rink, which he felt could be dangerous to the players. On impact, the

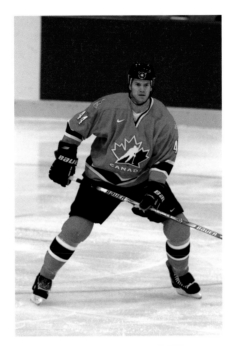

CHRIS PRONGER
Defense—shoots left
6'6" 220 lbs.
b. Dryden, Ontario,
October 10, 1974

glass partitions separated, to provide more of a cushion to the players. Unfortunately for Pronger, Cherry's concerns proved valid. After being checked hard into the end boards by Finnish forward Teemu Selanne, he went face-first into the glass, and his nose caught in between two partitions that closed in on his forehead, pinching his face between the glass. The result was a huge gash on his forehead. Luckily, the injury was not as serious as it could have been, but Pronger will carry an Olympic scar as a constant reminder.

Pronger was also the catalyst of what may have been the best play of the hockey tournament, which occurred in the championship game against the USA. Just moments after receiving a drop pass from Mario Lemieux, Pronger returned the pass toward number 66, who was streaking toward the front of the American goal. It appeared Lemieux was set to shoot, but he coyly allowed it go between his skates and right onto the waiting stick of linemate Paul Kariya. Most importantly, goaltender Mike Richter took the bait and left the far side of the net open for Kariya to whistle a shot into. That goal tied the game 1-1 and gave the Canadians an important boost.

Pronger first represented his country at the 1993 World Junior Championships, returning from Gavle, Sweden with a gold medal after scoring four points in seven games. The win marked the first in a string of five straight victories for Canada. Pronger was also part of the gold medal- winning team at the 1997 World Championships.

Pronger was chosen second overall in the 1993 NHL Entry Draft by the Hartford Whalers and was traded to St. Louis for 2002 Olympic teammate Brendan Shanahan on July 27, 1995. On September 29, 1997, just two weeks shy of his 23rd birthday, he was named the captain of the Blues, the youngest in franchise history.

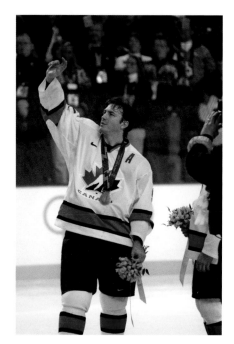

JOE SAKIC
Centre—shoots left
5'11" 195 lbs.
b. Burnaby, British Columbia,
July 7, 1969

It is often said that champions raise their level of play when the most is on the line. Joe Sakic of the Colorado Avalanche effectively proved that point at Salt Lake City, where he was without a doubt the main factor in Canada's securing its first Olympic men's hockey gold medal in half a century.

The 32-year-old Sakic was a dominant force in the thrilling 5-2 win over the United States, scoring two goals and two assists. "It was a great feeling to win the gold," Sakic said, smiling after the historic victory. "I've won the Stanley Cup, and now I've won here." The veteran centre truly has risen to the top at every level, from his minor league days in British Columbia and through his professional competition.

He first represented Canada at the 1988 World Junior tournament, helping his country return home with the gold medal. One of his teammates that year was fellow 2002 Olympic teammate Theoren Fleury. Ironically, the pair also tied for the WHL scoring title that year, each with 160 points. Sakic starred for Swift Cur-

rent and Fleury with Moose Jaw. Of course, Sakic was the main offensive force in Colorado's Stanley Cup championships in both 1996 and 2001 and was named the winner of the 1996 Conn Smythe Trophy.

Entering the gold medal game against the USA, Sakic had been Canada's top offensive star in Salt Lake. He finished as the team's scoring leader with seven points (four goals, three assists), tying American John LeClair for third spot, behind only Mats Sundin of Sweden and Brett Hull of the USA (who had nine and eight points, respectively). Sakic was named the tournament MVP

and was also Canada's lone Olympic All-Star selection. "It's a great honour," the always humble Sakic said. When asked if Wayne Gretzky deserved a gold medal for his tireless efforts in putting the team together, Sakic responded, "Sure he does—but he's not getting mine."

International competition runs deep for Sakic, whose parents emigrated from Croatia. He has also twice donned the maple leaf for his country at the World Championships, helping Canada to the silver in 1991 and gold in 1994. While he has enjoyed tremendous success, Sakic was also a member of the Canadian team that finished second at the World Cup of Hockey and fourth at the 1998 Olympics in Nagano.

Sakic was originally selected 15th overall by the Quebec Nordiques in the 1987 NHL Entry Draft. Some of his other individual NHL accomplishments include winning the Hart, Lady Byng, and Lester B. Pearson Trophies in 2001, and appearing in nine NHL All-Star Games. ❦

"I don't know if I've ever felt anything like this before." Those were the jubilant words from Team Canada forward Brendan Shanahan moments after he and his countrymen took gold at the Salt Lake City Olympics.

In the fall of 2001, when Team Canada management was putting together a list of candidates who would represent their country, it was not a given that Shanahan was going to be one of the players selected. A fast start to the NHL season brought a tremendous amount of attention to the 33-year-old Detroit Red Wings veteran, and he was one of the 23 players named to the team during a live television announcement from the Hockey Hall of Fame in Toronto on December 15, 2001.

Because the Canadian team was deep in offensive talent, Shanahan received limited ice time in several games, sharing shifts with the likes of Ryan Smyth and Michael Peca. He finished the 2002 Olympic tournament with one assist and always remained a vocal leader in the dressing room.

An emotional memory for Shanahan occurred right after Joe Sakic scored with 1:20 remaining in the third period in the gold medal game. "We could hear 'O, Canada'

BRENDAN SHANAHAN
Right Wing—shoots right
6'3" 220 lbs.
b. Mimico, Ontario,
January 23, 1969

being sung throughout the arena," he smiled. "It was an historic game for Canada, and we're all honoured to have been a part of it." What was not known until after the conclusion of the Olympics was that Shanahan played the final two games with a broken thumb, an injury he suffered in the 2-1 quarter-finals win over Finland.

Shanahan's international story began back in 1987 when he played at the World Junior Championships in Piestany, Czechoslovakia along with 2002 Olympic teammate Theoren Fleury. It was a tournament best remembered for its bench-

clearing brawl which ended the game between Canada and Russia and resulted in disqualification for both teams. It essentially cost Canada what would have been a gold medal. In six games, Shanahan had been an offensive spark, scoring four goals and seven points. Fellow 2002 Olympians Sergei Fedorov and Vladimir Malakhov played for the Russians that year.

Shanahan played on Canada's victorious 1991 Canada Cup team. In eight games, he contributed two goals. Another great international event came in 1994 when he scored seven points in six games in helping Canada to win its first World Championships gold medal in 33 years.

Shanahan was selected second overall in the 1987 NHL Entry Draft by the New Jersey Devils, where he played four years before signing with the St. Louis Blues as a free agent on July 25, 1991. He was traded to the Hartford Whalers for 2002 Olympic teammate Chris Pronger on July 27, 1995. At the 1997 Entry Draft, he was traded to the Detroit Red Wings with Brian Glynn for Paul Coffey, Keith Primeau, and a draft pick (Nikos Tselios). As a member of the Red Wings, Shanahan has won two Stanley Cups in 1997 and 1998.

RYAN SMYTH
Left Wing—shoots left
6'1" 195 lbs.
b. Banff, Alberta,
February 21, 1976

Wayne Gretzky, Kevin Lowe, and the coaches of Team Canada's Olympic hockey team all believed that Edmonton Oilers forward Ryan Smyth would excel on the large international ice because of his excellent skating and aggressive checking style. He did not disappoint at Salt Lake City. He proved to be a tireless worker, causing numerous turnovers in the opponent's end.

Smyth was the odd-man-out in the opening game against Sweden, a 5-2 loss for Canada. He was quickly inserted into Canada's second game against Germany and turned in a tremendous effort which earned him a spot in the lineup for the remaining four games of the Olympic tournament. In five games, Smyth contributed one assist.

The first time Smyth played for his country was in 1995 when Canada came away with the gold medal at the World Junior Championships in Red Deer, Alberta. "It was an incredible experience winning gold for my country with a great bunch of guys," Smyth said. Ed Jovanovski, a close friend of Smyth's and a teammate on the 2002 Olympic squad, was also a member of that 1995 junior club.

For three years in a row, beginning in 1999, Smyth represented Canada at the World Championships. Despite not winning a medal, the international experience was immeasurable. Many players say that having played in previous international competitions made the transition to the bigger Olympic ice surface easier to handle.

Coming out of junior with Moose Jaw of the WHL, Smyth was selected 6th overall by the Edmonton Oilers in the 1994 NHL Entry Draft. Known for his defensive checking abilities, he also proved he could play offensively as well, producing his best season in the NHL in 2000-01 when he recorded 70 points on 31 goals and 39 assists. ❦

Steve Yzerman was one of Canada's assistant captains at the 2002 Olympics in Salt Lake City, and his leadership qualities both on and off the ice proved to be an instrumental factor in propelling Canada to the gold medal victory over the United States.

At 36, Yzerman chose not to practice with the team between games at the Olympics. "I only play in the games," Yzerman joked to the media. "Actually, I'm a little bit sore [coming off the knee surgery] and I'm fine to play, but I'm better to take the rest." As it turned out, Yzerman was being exceptionally modest. Following the gold medal victory, he acknowledged he was by no means sure if he were going to be able to participate at all. It was evident something was wrong when he sat out the entire second period in the championship game after having played tremendously in the opening 20 minutes.

When he returned for the third period, Yzerman was again dominant, creating numerous scoring opportunities with linemate Joe Sakic. He picked up an assist on Jarome Iginla's third-period goal, giving Canada some breathing room at 4-2, with just under four minutes to play en route to the 5-2 victory. "You've got to give a lot of credit to Yzerman," said associate coach Jacques Martin. "He came here hurt and then played like there was no tomorrow. The guy was outstanding. He really was." In his own words, Yzerman admitted "I really wasn't sure [about playing], but

STEVE YZERMAN
Centre—shoots right
5'11" 185 lbs.
b. Cranbrook, British Columbia,
May 9, 1965

when I made the decision to come, I was committed. I just wanted to play my best and forget about the injury."

Throughout the entire Olympic tournament, Yzerman was consistently one of Canada's top offensive threats, averaging a point per game through the gold medal game and finishing with two goals and four assists. He equalled captain Mario Lemieux's output for second-best on the team, just one point behind Joe Sakic's team-leading seven.

Yzerman, of course, is no stranger to international hockey, first sporting the Team Canada sweater at the

1983 World Junior Championships in Leningrad, playing alongside 2002 Olympic captain Lemieux. In seven games, Yzerman had two goals and five points to help his country to the bronze medal. That was 19 years ago.

The next international competition for Yzerman came in 1984 when he was selected to play in the Canada Cup. At 19, he was one of the youngest players on the squad and saw only limited ice time in the four games he dressed. In 1985 and 1989, he was a member of the Canadian National Team that brought home silver at the World Championships. In 1989, he was named to the tournament All-Star Team after scoring five goals and 12 points in eight games. Yzerman followed that up in 1990 with an even stronger individual performance, scoring ten goals and 20 points in ten games and being named the tournament's top forward.

The next opportunity for Yzerman to appear on the international scene was at the 1996 World Cup of Hockey where he scored two goals and three points in six games. As captain of the Red Wings, Yzerman guided the club to two successive Stanley Cup championships in 1997 and 1998.

Yzerman was selected fourth overall in the 1983 NHL Entry Draft by the Detroit Red Wings after playing two years of junior hockey with the Peterborough Petes of the OHL. As a youngster, he played for a team that once went 143 games without a loss when he was in the lineup. ✢

DANA ANTAL
Forward—shoots right
5'7" 135 lbs.
b. Saskatoon, Saskatchewan,
April 19, 1977

KELLY BECHARD
Forward—shoots right
5'9" 145 lbs.
b. Sedley, Saskatchewan,
January 28, 1978

Kelly Bechard brought the experience of two World Championships (2000 and 2001) to her first Olympic competition. The hard working Bechard earned one assist during the tournament, but her tripping penalty late in third period of the game against Team USA had Bechard holding her breath. Just 23 seconds after she entered the penalty box, Karyn Bye of Team USA scored to make the score 3-2 Canada. Fortunately, Canada was able to hold the U.S. off the scoresheet the rest of the way to capture the gold medal.

Bechard is pursuing a degree in management at the University of Calgary and plays for the CIAU hockey team. In 1998, she was named to the CIAU's First All-Star Team and was presented the Award of Merit. She also plays for Calgary's Oval X-Treme.

Dana Antal has used her hockey career to travel the world. Between 1995 and 1997, Antal attended Cornell University, studying psychology. She was selected the Ivy League's rookie of the year in 1995-96 and led the Cornell Big Red in scoring both seasons she played there. In 1997-98, Antal played hockey in Switzerland. She later joined the Oval X-Treme while attending the University of Calgary.

Antal was a member of the Canadian National Women's Hockey Team that won the World Championship gold medal in 2001. She had been named to the team in 2000 as well but was unable to play because of an injury. Antal scored two goals and added an assist at the Olympic Games in Salt Lake City.

JENNIFER BOTTERILL
Forward—shoots left
5'9" 155 lbs.
b. Winnipeg, Manitoba,
May 1, 1979

A phenomenal athlete, Jennifer Botterill is surrounded by successful competitors. Her mother, Doreen, competed in speedskating at the 1964 and 1968 Olympics. Her father, Cal, was once a member of the Canadian National Team and spent time in the Boston Bruins' system. Older brother Jason was a first-round draft pick of the NHL's Dallas Stars.

But Jennifer Botterill doesn't need to ride anyone's coattails. Playing for prestigious Harvard University while pursuing a degree in psychology, she helped Harvard win the U.S. College Hockey Championship in 1998-99. In 2000-01, Botterill set a United States college hockey record—men and women—by scoring a point or more in 80 consecutive games.

She represented her country at the 1998 Nagano Olympics, helping Canada earn a silver medal. At 18, she was the youngest player on the team. The team took the gold at the World Championships in 1999, 2000, and 2001 with Botterill on the team.

In Salt Lake City, Botterill had a strong tournament. She scored three goals and three assists. ❧

THERESE BRISSON
Defense—shoots right
5'7" 150 lbs.
b. Dollard-des-Ormeaux, Quebec,
October 5, 1966

The second oldest member of Team Canada's gold medal-winning team, Therese Brisson is also one of the most decorated. She has five World Championship gold medals (1994, 1997, 1999, 2000, 2001), a silver medal from Nagano's 1998 Olympic Winter Games, and now her shiny new gold medal from Salt Lake City.

Brisson began her road to hockey stardom at Montreal's Concordia University. While studying kinesiology, she was named female athlete of the year in both 1988 and 1989. So profound were Brisson's contributions to Concordia's athletic program that she was inducted into Concordia's Sports Hall of Fame in 1997.

Brisson is a born leader. In 1994, the rookie was named an all-star defenseman at the World Championships. She captained the women's National Team to gold medals in 1999, 2000, and 2001.

A former professor of kinesiology at the University of New Brunswick, Therese Brisson led all Canadian defensemen in scoring at the 2002 Olympic tournament. She scored two goals and three assists for five points in the five games played. ❧

CASSIE CAMPBELL
Forward—shoots left
5'8" 140 lbs.
b. Brampton, Ontario,
November 22, 1973

ISABELLE CHARTRAND
Defense—shoots left
5'5" 130 lbs.
b. Anjou, Quebec,
April 20, 1978

Having participated in the Salt Lake City Olympics before her 24th birthday, Isabelle Chartrand was one of the younger members of the gold medal-winning Canadian Women's Team. Her preparation was appropriate —she won a gold medal with Team Canada at the 2001 World Championships.

Chartrand is attending St. Lawrence University in Canton, New York. A member of the ECAC hockey team, she was named rookie of the week for January 15, 2001.

Chartrand contributed two goals and an assist to the potent Canadian attack in Salt Lake. ❧

The charismatic captain of Team Canada led the team to gold at the 2002 Olympic Winter Games. Campbell scored two goals and one assist, but her significance went far beyond statistics. Her confidence permeated through the dressing room—it's hard not to respect a veteran who has earned five gold medals and an Olympic silver medal.

Campbell first participated in the World Championships as part of Canada's 1994 team. Earning a gold that year, the team duplicated the feat in 1997, 1999, 2000, and 2001. In 1997, she was named to the All-Star Team on defense. She was an assistant captain for Canada in '97, '99, 2000, and 2001.

Campbell earned her honours degree in sociology from the University of Guelph. While playing with Guelph's hockey team, she was named to the second All-Star Team in 1993 and made the First All-Star Team in 1996. In fact, in 1996, she was named the University of Guelph's sportswoman of the year.

Not only a dominant and inspiring player, Campbell is one of the most recognized athletes in Canada. ❧

LORI DUPUIS
Forward—shoots left
5'8" 165 lbs.
b. Cornwall, Ontario,
November 14, 1972

After playing minor hockey in Cornwall, Dupuis attended the University of Toronto from 1991 to 1997. While earning an Honours B. A. in French and Geography, she was playing hockey for the U of T Blues. The team won four championships during the six years she was on the team. She also captained the team for her final three seasons.

In 1996, Dupuis was named female athlete of the year at the University of Toronto. Astonishingly, she repeated the honour in 1997.

Dupuis won gold medals with the Canadian National Women's Team in 1997, 1999, and 2000. In 1998, she was part of the silver medal Canadian women's hockey team in Nagano, Japan. In Salt Lake City, Dupuis scored a goal and earned an assist.

One of eight children, Dupuis plays for the Brampton Thunder of the National Women's Hockey League. Along with teammate Jayna Hefford, she also runs a hockey school for girls and women.

DANIELLE GOYETTE
Forward—shoots left
5'7" 150 lbs.
b. St-Nazaire, Quebec,
January 30, 1966

The veteran forward has participated in six World Championships as part of the Canadian women's hockey team and has won a gold medal each time out. Goyette played at the World Championships in 1992, 1994, 1997, 1999, 2000, and 2001. She was also part of the Canadian delegation at the Olympic Winter Games in Nagano in 1998. In that tournament, Goyette was the leading goal scorer.

In 2002, Team Canada's oldest player tied Hayley Wickenheiser for most points. Both scored ten points on their way to an Olympic gold medal. Goyette scored three goals in total, including two in the 7-0 victory over Russia on February 13. She also led the tournament in assists with seven.

Goyette learned a great deal about competition in her St. Nazaire home. She is one of eight children, seven of whom are girls. Besides excelling in hockey, Goyette has also won a World Championship as a member of the Canadian fastball team.

GERALDINE HEANEY
Defense—shoots right
5'8" 140 lbs.
b. Northern Ireland,
October 1, 1967

JAYNA HEFFORD
Forward—shoots right
5'5" 140 lbs.
born Kingston, Ontario,
May 14, 1977

Jayna Hefford was a member of Team Canada in 1998, winning a silver medal in Nagano, Japan. But in Salt Lake City in 2002, she was determined to win the gold medal. In the February 19 romp over Sweden, Hefford scored one goal and added three assists to lead Canada to an 11-0 victory. In the gold medal game versus the United States, it was Hefford's goal with one second remaining in the second period that proved to be not only the game-winning goal, but the gold medal-winner as well. Through the tournament, Hefford scored three goals and added three assists.

Hefford has four gold medals already, earned in the four World Championships in which she has participated—1994, 1999, 2000, 2001. In both 1999 and 2000, she was Team Canada's leading scorer. Her two third-period goals in the 2000 championship game pushed the contest into overtime, allowing Canada to win gold once again. Hefford plays with the Brampton Thunder in the WNHL. ✦

With the gold medal victory at the 2002 Olympic Winter Games, Geraldine Heaney became the first Canadian hockey player—man or woman—to play on seven World Championship teams and to win both an Olympic gold and silver medal. The savvy veteran won gold for Canada in 1990, 1992, 1994, 1997, 1999, 2000, and 2001. In '92 and '94, she was selected best defenseman in the tournament.

But Heaney is not just a veteran of Team Canada's competitions. She has played for North York's Beatrice Aeros of the Women's National Hockey League since the team's inception 18 years ago.

Before travelling to Nagano, Japan in 1998, Heaney had the Olympic rings tattooed on her hip. It was an omen of things to come. She now is the proud owner of a silver medal from Nagano and a gold from Salt Lake City. At the 2002 Olympic Winter Games, Heaney was stalwart on defense and also assisted on three goals. ✦

BECKY KELLAR
Defense—shoots left
5'7" 150 lbs.
b. Hagersville, Ontario,
January 1, 1975

This New Year's baby is anything but new to accolades. Becky Kellar played four seasons with the Brown University Bears from 1993 to 1997. In her second season at the distinguished Ivy League university, Kellar scored 20 goals and 29 assists in just 23 games. In 1995-96, she was selected the league's most valuable player. Kellar earned both her Bachelor of Arts degree in Psychology and her teaching certificate. Following her final year at Brown, Kellar was awarded the Academic All-Ivy in 1997, honouring her outstanding scholastic and athletic achievements.

The 2002 Olympics were her second Games. She was part of the Canadian women's silver medal team in Nagano Japan in 1998. She has also been a member of three consecutive World Championship Canadian teams—1999, 2000, and 2001. In Salt Lake, Kellar collected one assist and served six minutes in penalties

A member of the Beatrice Aeros team in the Women's National Hockey League, Kellar is attending Waterloo's Wilfrid Laurier University to work on her Master's Degree. ✦

CAROLINE OUELLETTE
Forward—shoots left
5'11" 170 lbs.
b. Montreal, Quebec,
May 25, 1979

To excel in sports, one must learn focus and discipline. Ouellette has trained to ensure her focus and discipline are always at their zenith. In the fall of 2000, she graduated from the National Police Academy in Quebec. Prior to attending the Police Academy, Ouellete studied sociology at Montreal's Concordia University.

Part of three gold medal-winning Canadian women's hockey teams, Ouellette was a forward at the World Championships in 1999, 2000, and 2001. Participating in her first Olympics, she was a key contributor to Canada's potent offense. She scored two goals and four assists for six points during the five-game tournament. In the 7-0 victory over Russia, Ouellette had two assists, and she collected a goal and an assist in the February 16 drubbing of Sweden. During the gold medal game versus the United States, Ouellete scored one of Canada's three goals.

Ouellette is a member of the Wingstar de Montreal women's hockey team. But hockey is not Ouellette's only game. She played on Quebec's fastball team at the 1997 Canada Summer Games. ✦

CHERIE PIPER
Forward—shoots right
5'5" 165 lbs.
b. Scarborough, Ontario,
June 29, 1981

Cherie Piper was the last player named to Team Canada in 2002, and her selection came amidst much controversy. Although she had been practising with the team, coach Daniele Sauvageau followed a hunch and dropped veteran Nancy Drolet from the lineup in order to get the offense of Cherie Piper onto the team. Although Drolet officially protested the decision, she was overruled, and Cherie Piper became a full-fledged member of the Canadian National Women's Team.

Her selection by Sauvageau was astute, as Piper worked incredibly hard game after game. She finished the tournament with three goals and two assists... and a gold medal.

The youngest member of Team Canada, Piper was selected her high school's athlete of the year for 1999-2000. And while excelling in sports, she continued to be an honours student.

Piper also plays with North York's Beatrice Aeros. ❦

CHERYL POUNDER
Defense—shoots right
5'6" 145 lbs.
b. Mississauga, Ontario,
June 21, 1976

Although this was Cheryl Pounder's first Olympic experience, it certainly wasn't her first international competition. Pounder had four gold medals in her collection already, having been part of the winning Canadian women's hockey teams at the 1994, 1999, 2000, and 2001 World Championships.

In Salt Lake City, Pounder proved that contributions weren't exclusive to the scoresheet. The only member of Team Canada to miss registering a point (besides single-game goaltender Sami Jo Small), she was, nonetheless, an important part of Team Canada. Her solid defensive play helped Canada earn three shutouts, holding the competition to just five goals against in as many games. Her plus-minus was a healthy +8, second only to Colleen Sostorics (+11) and tied with Geraldine Heaney and Cassie Campbell.

While earning her degree in kinesiology at the Wilfrid Laurier University in Waterloo, Ontario, Pounder was named female athlete of the year in 1997-98. ❦

TAMMY LEE SHEWCHUK
Forward—shoots right
5'4" 140 lbs.
b. St-Laurent, Quebec,
December 31, 1977

Tammy Lee Shewchuk completed an extraordinary college career playing with Harvard. During her four years in Boston, she became the NCAA's all-time leading scorer. She holds the records for career goals (160), career assists (147), and career points (307). In 1998-99, Shewchuk was named a First Team All-America and led Harvard to the College Hockey Championship. She also earned Harvard's John Dooley Award for combining sportsmanship, enthusiasm, and devotion to hockey.

Even as a child, young Tammy Lee was breaking records. As a 14-year-old, this New Year's Eve baby was the first female non-goaltender to play in the world-renowned Quebec PeeWee Tournament.

Shewchuk earned two points during the Olympics at Salt Lake, scoring a goal and adding an assist. It was her first Olympic experience, although she has won gold medals with Canada's 2000 and 2001 World Championships teams. ❧

SAMI JO SMALL
Goaltender—catches left
5'7" 187 lbs.
b. Winnipeg, Manitoba,
March 25, 1976

Small has been selected to represent Canada at the World Championships three times. In both 1999 and 2000, she not only led Team Canada to gold medals, she was also named All-Star goaltender in both tournaments. In 2001, she again was on the gold medal-winning Canadian team.

At the 2002 Games in Salt Lake, Small started game two against the Russians, shutting them out decisively in a 7-0 Canadian win on February 13. Facing just six shots, Small needed to maintain her focus as her teammates dominated the Russians. It was the only game in which Small played in Salt Lake City.

Small graduated from Stanford University in 1999 with a degree in mechanical engineering. While attending this prestigious U.S. university, Small played on the men's hockey team. She was also a member of Stanford's track team for four years. Since 1999-2000, Small has played for the Brampton Thunder in the National Women's Hockey League. During the 2000-2001 season, she scored a goal from her goaltending position. ❧

COLLEEN SOSTORICS
Defense—shoots right
5'4" 174 lbs.
b. Kennedy, Saskatchewan,
December 17, 1979

Although Sostorics is not very tall, competitors quickly found that getting past her was a real challenge. The solid defender played wonderful defensively at the 2002 Olympic Winter Games and contributed two assists to the offense.

Relatively new to Team Canada, Sostorics enjoyed her first Olympic experience, though she was also on the gold medal-winning Canadian Team at the 2001 World Championships.

Besides playing hockey with Team Canada and the Oval X-Treme out of Calgary, Sostorics excels at many sports. In both 1994 and 1995, she was named Most Valuable Women's Fastball Player at the Saskatchewan Provincial Tournaments. In 1997, she won a triple crown of sorts: she was on the provincial championship fastball, soccer, and hockey teams. Colleen Sostorics is studying economics at the University of Calgary. ❧

KIM ST. PIERRE
Goaltender —catches left
5'8" 150 lbs.
b. Chateauguay, Quebec,
December 14, 1978

The dominant goaltender at the 2002 Olympics, Kim St. Pierre earned two shutouts in the four games she played in Salt Lake City. In fact, St. Pierre played 139 minutes and 35 seconds of shutout goaltending before Finland's Tiia Reima broke the scoreless streak during Canada's fifth game, on February 19.

St. Pierre was selected Canada's starting netminder to open these Olympics, shutting out Kazakhstan 7-0 on February 11. She led Canada to an 11-0 triumph over Sweden on February 16. Three days later, Canada defeated Finland 7-3. In the deciding game, held February 21 against USA, St. Pierre backstopped her team to a thrilling 3-2 victory to claim Olympic gold for Canada. In four games played, St. Pierre allowed just five goals.

Although the 2002 Games were her first Olympic experience, she played in the 1999, 2000, and 2001 World Championships, helping Canada win the gold medal at each.

St. Pierre is working on a degree in kinesiology at Montreal's McGill University while playing for the women's hockey team. ❧

VICKY SUNOHARA
Forward—shoots left
5'7" 170 lbs.
b. Scarborough, Ontario,
May 18, 1970

Although others on Team Canada have participated in more World Championships, only Vicky Sunohara can claim a gold medal at the 1990 tournament. As a 20-year-old, Sunohara was already turning hockey heads when she helped the Canadian National Women's Team win a gold medal more than a decade ago. In fact, she has helped Canada earn gold medals at the World Championships in 1997, 1999, 2000, and 2001. The 2002 Olympics were the second for Sunohara—she played for Canada in Nagano in 1998, winning the silver medal.

Sunohara's maturity helped Canada claim the gold medal at the 2002 Games in Salt Lake. In game one, versus Kazakhstan, the veterans Sunohara and Wickenheiser both scored two goals to lead Canada to a resounding 7-0 win. Sunohara scored another two during the tournament. Her four goals and two assists gave her six points.

In 1988-89, Sunohara attended Northeastern University. Northeastern won the ECAC championship that season, and she scored 51 goals and 23 assists in 25 games.

HAYLEY WICKENHEISER
Forward—shoots right
5'9" 170 lbs.
b. Shaunavon, Saskatchewan,
December 8, 1978

Few will ever forget the sight of Team Canada assistant captain Hayley Wickenheiser clutching her son, Noah, as she skated around the E-Center celebrating a gold medal for Canada's National Women's Team. It had been a sensational tournament for Wickenheiser. She was named to the Olympic All-Star Team, leading all players with seven goals. Her three assists gave her a point total of ten points, the same number as teammate Danielle Goyette, to lead the tournament as well. "Wick" scored two goals against Kazakhstan in the opening game 7-0 victory on February 11. She scored two against Finland as well, leading Canada to a 7-3 win.

The Salt Lake City Olympic Winter Games are the third Olympics in which Wickenheiser has competed. In 1998, the 19-year old helped Canada win a silver medal in women's hockey. But, at the 2000 Summer Games in Sydney, she competed on the Women's Softball Team. In addition, Wickenheiser has competed at the World Championships as part of the Canadian National Women's Team in 1994 (she was just 15 years old), 1997, 1999, and 2000. Each time, Canada won the gold medal.

Coach Daniele Sauvageau (top) pops a bottle of celebratory bubbly while Hayley Wickenheiser (right) receives her special medal for being named the women's MVP of Salt Lake 2002.

(top, left to right) Colleen Sostorics, Lori Dupuis, and Tammy Lee Shewchuk show their medals while (below) Shewchuk and Dana Antal do the same moments later.

Danielle Goyette shows off her medal during the dressing room festivities.

Isabelle Chartrand (left) and Colleen Sostorics share in a bottle of champagne to stay in the spirit of the moment.

After their win at the E-Center, the women's team went across the street to the Hale Center
where the Stanley Cup and other trophies from the Hockey Hall of Fame had been on display
during the Olympics. Here they had a chance to get close to Lord Stanley's trophy.

Captain fantastic, Mario Lemieux, pops open the champers to start the celebrations in the men's dressing room following their 5-2 win over USA in the men's finals.

Ryan Smyth, Eric Lindros, and Owen Nolan give the champions' salute during the post-game revelry in their dressing room.

Coach Pat Quinn adds his name to a wall in the team's dressing room used for everyone's signature.

Paul Kariya (left) and Michael Peca show their gold, two men who will certainly be on the team in 2006 if NHLers play in the Olympics again.

The Dallas connection of (left to right) Joe Nieuwendyk, Ken Hitchcock, and Ed Belfour pose for a group shot after the win.

The Irish threesome of Owen Nolan, Pat Quinn, and Brendan Shanahan clown around for photographers.

The most dominant line of 2002— (left to right) Simon Gagne, Joe Sakic, and Jarome Iginla.

(top, left to right) Adam Foote, Jacques Martin, Owen Nolan, and Joe Sakic share a hug while (below) Al MacInnis, Eric Lindros, and Rob Blake sit back and enjoy their victory.

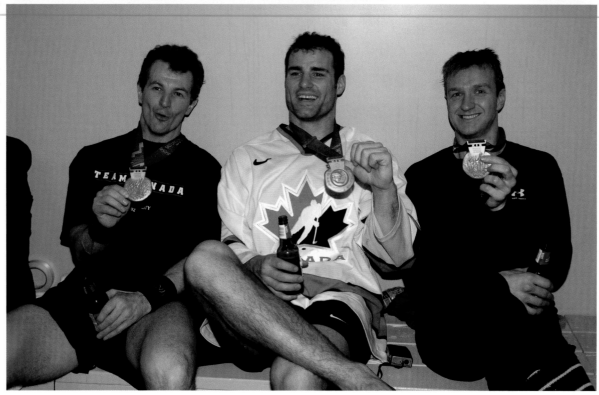

During a brief lull in the hectic Olympics schedule, the men's and women's teams got together for a group photo outside the E-Center, home to most of the games at the Salt Lake Olympics.

Summary of Results — Men

PRELIMINARY ROUND

Group A
	GP	W	L	T	GF	GA	P
Germany	3	3	0	0	10	3	6
Latvia	3	1	1	1	11	12	3*
Slovakia	3	1	1	1	9	11	3
Austria	3	0	3	0	6	10	0

*finished second because of better goal differential

February 9	Germany	3	Slovakia	0
	Latvia	4	Austria	2
February 10	Germany	3	Austria	2
	Latvia	6	Slovakia	6
February 12	Slovakia	3	Austria	2
	Germany	4	Latvia	1

Group B
	GP	W	L	T	GF	GA	P
Belarus	3	2	1	0	5	3	4*
Ukraine	3	2	1	0	9	5	4
Switzerland	3	1	1	1	7	9	3
France	3	0	2	1	6	10	1

*finished first because of head-to-head result with Ukraine

February 9	Belarus	1	Ukraine	0
	Switzerland	3	France	3
February 11	Ukraine	5	Switzerland	2
	Belarus	3	France	1
February 13	Switzerland	2	Belarus	1
	Ukraine	4	France	2

CLASSIFICATION GAMES

February 14	Switzerland	4	Austria	1
	Latvia	9	Ukraine	2
	Slovakia	7	France	1

FINAL ROUND

Group C
	GP	W	L	T	GF	GA	P
Sweden	3	3	0	0	14	4	6
Czech	3	1	1	1	12	7	3*
Canada	3	1	1	1	8	10	3
Germany	3	0	3	0	5	18	0

*finished second because of better goal differential

February 15	Sweden	5	Canada	2
	Czech	8	Germany	2
February 17	Canada	3	Germany	2
	Sweden	2	Czech	1
February 18	Canada	3	Czech	3
	Sweden	7	Germany	1

Group D
	GP	W	L	T	GF	GA	P
USA	3	3	0	0	16	3	6
Russia	3	2	0	1	11	7	5
Finland	3	1	2	0	9	10	2
Belarus	3	0	3	0	6	22	0

February 15	Russia	6	Belarus	4
	USA	6	Finland	0
February 16	Finland	8	Belarus	1
	Russia	2	USA	2
February 18	Finland	3	Russia	1
	USA	8	Belarus	1

QUARTER-FINALS
February 20	Canada	2	Finland	1
	Belarus	4	Sweden	3
	Russia	1	Czech	0
	USA	5	Germany	0

SEMI-FINALS
February 22	Canada	7	Belarus	1
	USA	3	Russia	2

BRONZE MEDAL GAME
February 23	Russia	7	Belarus	2

GOLD MEDAL GAME
February 24	Canada	5	USA	2

PRELIMINARY ROUND

Group A

	GP	W	L	T	GF	GA	P
Canada	3	3	0	0	25	0	6
Sweden	3	2	1	0	10	13	4
Russia	3	1	2	0	6	11	2
Kazakhstan	3	0	3	0	1	18	0

February 11	Canada	7	Kazakhstan	0
	Sweden	3	Russia	2
February 13	Canada	7	Russia	0
	Sweden	7	Kazakhstan	0
February 15	Russia	4	Kazakhstan	1
February 16	Canada	11	Sweden	0

Group B

	GP	W	L	T	GF	GA	P
USA	3	3	0	0	27	1	6
Finland	3	2	1	0	7	6	4
Germany	3	0	2	1	6	18	1*
China	3	0	2	1	6	21	1

* finished third because of better goal differential

February 12	Finland	4	China	0
	USA	10	Germany	0
February 14	Finland	3	Germany	1
	USA	12	China	1
February 16	Germany	5	China	5
	USA	5	Finland	0

CLASSIFICATION GAMES

February 17	Russia	4	China	1
	Germany	4	Kazakhstan	0

5th place game

February 19	Russia	5	Germany	0

7th place game

February 19	China	2	Kazakhstan	1
	(Overtime)			

SEMI-FINALS

February 19	Canada	7	Finland	3
	USA	4	Sweden	0

BRONZE MEDAL GAME

February 21	Sweden	2	Finland	1

GOLD MEDAL GAME

February 21	Canada	3	USA	2

Final Statistics — Men

AUSTRIA

#	Name	Pos	GP	G	A	P	Pim
4	UNTERLUGGAUER, Gerhard	D	4	2	0	2	4
12	TRATTNIG, Matthias	F	4	1	1	2	2
26	WHEELDON, Simon	F	4	1	1	2	4
29	PERTHALER, Christian	F	3	0	2	2	0
11	RESSMANN, Gerald	F	4	1	0	1	2
15	SETZINGER, Oliver	F	4	1	0	1	2
9	SEARLE, Thomas	D	4	1	0	1	4
74	KALT, Dieter	F	4	1	0	1	6
6	LAVOIE, Joseph	D	4	0	1	1	2
10	BRANDNER, Christoph	F	4	0	1	1	2
18	SALFI, Kent	F	4	0	1	1	2
27	KROMP, Wolfgang	F	4	0	1	1	4
24	LANZINGER, Gunther	F	4	0	1	1	14
38	DIVIS, Reinhard	G	4	0	0	0	0
96	KASPER, Peter	D	4	0	0	0	0
21	SCHADEN, Mario	F	4	0	0	0	0
13	LUKAS, Robert	D	4	0	0	0	0
31	DALPIAZ, Claus	G	4	0	0	0	0
25	SUTTNIG, Michael	G	4	0	0	0	0
22	HOHENBERGER, Martin	F	4	0	0	0	0
16	POCK, Thomas	F	4	0	0	0	2
47	ULRICH, Martin	D	4	0	0	0	4
32	LAKOS, Andre	D	4	0	0	0	6

#	In Goal	GP	Mins	GA	GAA	SO
38	DIVIS, Reinhard	4	238:21	12	3.02	0

BELARUS

#	Name	Pos	GP	G	A	P	Pim
32	PANKOV, Dmitry	F	9	3	1	4	2
29	TSYPLAKOV, Vladimir	F	8	1	3	4	4
3	KHMYL, Oleg	D	9	1	3	4	0
23	SALEI, Ruslan	D	6	2	1	3	4
24	DUDIK, Dmitri	F	9	2	1	3	6
11	BEKBULATOV, Vadim	F	9	1	2	3	8
13	KOVALEV, Andrei	F	9	1	2	3	12
30	KOPAT, Vladimir	D	8	1	1	2	4
17	KALYUZHNY, Aleksei	F	9	1	1	2	0
37	RASSOLKO, Andrei	F	9	1	1	2	0
5	ROMANOV, Oleg	D	9	1	1	2	2
14	PANKOV, Vasily	F	9	1	1	2	4
18	ANTONENKO, Oleg	F	9	1	1	2	8
21	MIKULCHIK, Oleg	D	9	1	0	1	14
16	SKABELKA, Andrei	F	2	0	1	1	0
6	MATUSHKIN, Igor	D	9	0	1	1	0
27	ZHURIK, Aleksandr	D	9	0	1	1	6
26	STAS, Sergei	D	9	0	1	1	16
28	KOLTSOV, Konstantin	F	2	0	0	0	0
19	ZANKAVETS, Eduard	F	4	0	0	0	0
31	MEZIN, Andrei	G	9	0	0	0	0
2	SHABANOV, Sergei	G	9	0	0	0	0
33	FATIKOV, Leonid	G	9	0	0	0	0
9	ANDRIEVSKY, Aleksandr	F	9	0	0	0	4
4	MAKRITSKY, Alexandr	D	9	0	0	0	10

#	In Goal	GP	Mins	GA	GAA	SO
2	SHABANOV, Sergei	6	230:05	14	3.65	1
31	MEZIN, Andrei	7	309:55	28	5.42	0

CANADA

#	Name	Pos	GP	G	A	P	Pim
91	SAKIC, Joe	F	6	4	3	7	0
66	LEMIEUX, Mario	F	5	2	4	6	0
19	YZERMAN, Steve	F	6	2	4	6	2
12	IGINLA, Jarome	F	6	3	1	4	0
9	KARIYA, Paul	F	6	3	1	4	0
21	GAGNE, Simon	F	6	1	3	4	0
4	BLAKE, Rob	D	6	1	2	3	2
11	NOLAN, Owen	F	6	0	3	3	2
55	JOVANOVSKI, Ed	D	6	0	3	3	4
3	BREWER, Eric	D	6	2	0	2	2
25	NIEUWENDYK, Joe	F	6	1	1	2	0
27	NIEDERMAYER, Scott	D	6	1	1	2	4
37	PECA, Mike	F	6	0	2	2	2
74	FLEURY, Theo	F	6	0	2	2	6
52	FOOTE, Adam	D	6	1	0	1	2
88	LINDROS, Eric	F	6	1	0	1	8
14	SHANAHAN, Brendan	F	6	1	0	1	0
94	SMYTH, Ryan	F	6	0	1	1	0
44	PRONGER, Chris	D	6	0	1	1	2
20	BELFOUR, Ed	G	5	0	0	0	0
30	BRODEUR, Martin	G	6	0	0	0	0
31	JOSEPH, Curtis	G	6	0	0	0	0
2	MACINNIS, Al	D	6	0	0	0	8

#	In Goal	GP	Mins	GA	GAA	SO
30	BRODEUR, Martin	5	300:00	9	1.80	0
31	JOSEPH, Curtis	1	60:00	5	5.00	0

CZECH

#	Name	Pos	GP	G	A	P	Pim
68	JAGR, Jaromir	F	4	2	3	5	4
9	HAVLAT, Martin	F	4	3	1	4	27
30	DOPITA, Jiri	F	4	2	2	4	2
20	LANG, Robert	F	4	1	2	3	2
26	RUCINSKY, Martin	F	4	0	3	3	2
25	ELIAS, Patrik	F	4	1	1	2	0
17	SYKORA, Petr	F	4	1	0	1	0
24	HEJDUK, Milan	F	4	1	0	1	0
21	REICHEL, Robert	F	4	1	0	1	2
13	KUBINA, Pavel	D	4	0	1	1	0
4	HAMRLIK, Roman	D	4	0	1	1	2
15	KABERLE, Tomas	D	4	0	1	1	2
39	HASEK, Dominik	G	4	0	0	0	0
41	SKOULA, Martin	D	4	0	0	0	0
6	SPACEK, Jaroslav	D	4	0	0	0	0
38	HRDINA, Jan	F	4	0	0	0	0
29	SYKORA, Michal	D	4	0	0	0	0
23	CECHMANEK, Roman	G	4	0	0	0	0
19	DVORAK, Radek	F	4	0	0	0	0
16	CAJANEK, Petr	F	4	0	0	0	0
10	PATERA, Pavel	F	4	0	0	0	2
42	SMEHLIK, Richard	D	4	0	0	0	4

#	In Goal	GP	Mins	GA	GAA	SO
39	HASEK, Dominik	4	239:00	8	2.01	0

FINLAND

#	Name	Pos	GP	G	A	P	Pim
8	SELANNE, Teemu	F	4	3	0	3	2
12	JOKINEN, Olli	F	4	2	1	3	0
16	HAGMAN, Niklas	F	4	1	2	3	0
17	KALLIO, Tomi	F	4	1	2	3	2
26	LEHTINEN, Jere	F	4	1	2	3	2
24	KAPANEN, Sami	F	4	1	2	3	4
44	NIINIMAA, Janne	D	4	0	3	3	2
22	ELORANTA, Mikko	F	4	2	0	2	2
7	BERG, Aki-Petteri	D	4	1	0	1	2
6	VAANANEN, Ossi	D	2	0	1	1	0
21	LUMME, Jyrki	D	4	0	1	1	0
14	HELMINEN, Raimo	F	4	0	1	1	0
27	NUMMINEN, Teppo	D	4	0	1	1	0
4	TIMONEN, Kimmo	D	4	0	1	1	2
36	YLONEN, Juha	F	4	0	1	1	2
10	NIEMINEN, Ville	D	4	0	1	1	2
30	NURMINEN, Pasi	G	4	0	0	0	0
5	SALO, Sami	D	4	0	0	0	0
35	HURME, Jani	G	4	0	0	0	0
42	LIND, Juha	F	4	0	0	0	0
31	MARKKANEN, Jussi	G	4	0	0	0	0
37	RUUTU, Jarkko	F	4	0	0	0	4
41	AALTO, Antti	F	4	0	0	0	4

#	In Goal	GP	Mins	GA	GAA	SO
30	NURMINEN, Pasi	1	60:00	1	1.00	0
35	HURME, Jani	3	179:10	9	3.01	0

FRANCE

#	Name	Pos	GP	G	A	P	Pim
12	BOZON, Philippe	F	4	3	3	6	2
9	ROZENTHAL, Maurice	F	4	4	1	5	2
23	MORTAS, Anthony	F	4	0	1	1	2
3	BACHET, Vincent	D	4	0	1	1	4
10	MEUNIER, Laurent	F	4	0	1	1	6
1	HUET, Cristobal	G	3	0	0	0	0
8	BRIAND, Arnaud	F	3	0	0	0	0
27	AMAR, Baptiste	D	4	0	0	0	0
31	ROLLAND, Patrick	G	4	0	0	0	0
30	LHENRY, Fabrice	G	4	0	0	0	0
28	GRAS, Laurent	F	4	0	0	0	0
25	AIMONETTO, Richard	F	4	0	0	0	0
11	ROZENTHAL, Francois	F	4	0	0	0	0
16	BESSE, Guillaume	F	4	0	0	0	0
26	POURTANEL, Benoit	D	4	0	0	0	0
20	BONNARD, Jean-Francois	D	4	0	0	0	2
13	DEWOLF, Karl	D	4	0	0	0	2
24	PEREZ, Denis	D	4	0	0	0	4
6	BACHELET, Benoit	F	4	0	0	0	4
7	BARIN, Stephane	F	4	0	0	0	4
14	TREILLE, Yorrick	F	4	0	0	0	4
22	ZWIKEL, Jonathan	F	4	0	0	0	4
2	CARRIOU, Allan	D	4	0	0	0	6

#	In Goal	GP	Mins	GA	GAA	SO
1	HUET, Cristobal	3	178:41	10	3.36	0
31	ROLLAND, Patrick	1	60:00	7	7.00	0

Final Statistics — Men

GERMANY

#	Name	Pos	GP	G	A	P	Pim
48	SOCCIO, Leonard	F	7	3	3	6	8
49	KATHAN, Klaus	F	7	3	2	5	0
21	USTORF, Stefan	F	7	2	1	3	2
81	MACKAY, Mark	F	7	0	3	3	2
18	LOTH, Andreas	F	7	2	0	2	0
17	HECHT, Jochen	F	4	1	1	2	2
84	SEIDENBERG, Dennis	D	7	1	1	2	4
75	MORCZINIETZ, Andreas	F	3	0	2	2	0
27	ABSTREITER, Tobias	F	7	0	2	2	0
20	RUMRICH, Jurgen	F	7	1	0	1	0
22	REICHEL, Martin	F	7	1	0	1	0
83	BENDA, Jan	F	7	1	0	1	2
12	LUDEMANN, Mirko	D	4	0	1	1	0
11	STURM, Marco	F	5	0	1	1	0
13	SCHUBERT, Christoph	D	7	0	1	1	6
41	KUNCE, Daniel	D	7	0	1	1	43
6	MAYR, Jorg	D	1	0	0	0	0
80	MULLER, Robert	G	2	0	0	0	0
33	SELIGER, Marc	G	6	0	0	0	0
47	KUNAST, Christian	G	6	0	0	0	0
26	KREUTZER, Daniel	F	7	0	0	0	0
16	HYNES, Wayne	F	7	0	0	0	6
31	RENZ, Andreas	D	7	0	0	0	8
10	EHRHOFF, Christian	D	7	0	0	0	8
36	GOLDMANN, Erich	D	7	0	0	0	27

#	In Goal	GP	Mins	GA	GAA	SO
33	SELIGER, Marc	6	302:11	15	2.98	1
80	MULLER, Robert	2	78:15	4	3.07	0
47	KUNAST, Christian	2	39:30	7	10.63	0

LATVIA

#	Name	Pos	GP	G	A	P	Pim
12	MACIJEVSKIS, Aleksandrs	F	4	2	3	5	0
17	NIZIVIJS, Aleksandrs	F	4	2	3	5	2
8	FANDULS, Vyacheslavs	F	4	4	0	4	2
5	BONDAREVS, Igors	D	4	2	2	4	0
20	VITOLINS, Harijs	F	4	2	2	4	0
18	OZOLINSH, Sandis	D	1	0	4	4	0
29	CIPRUSS, Aigars	F	4	1	2	3	0
28	MATICINS, Sergejs	F	4	1	2	3	2
14	TAMBIJEVS, Leonids	F	4	1	2	3	2
21	KERCS, Aleksandrs	F	4	0	3	3	2
13	PANTELEJEVS, Gregorijs	F	4	2	0	2	2
27	SEMJONOVS, Aleksandrs	F	4	1	1	2	2
9	BELAVSKIS, Aleksandrs	F	4	1	1	2	4
22	SOROKINS, Olegs	D	4	0	2	2	4
23	TRIBUNCOVS, Atvars	D	4	1	0	1	8
15	ASTASENKO, Kaspars	D	3	0	1	1	0
11	SENINS, Sergejs	F	4	0	1	1	4
1	IRBE, Arturs	G	1	0	0	0	0
7	SKRASTINS, Karlis	D	1	0	0	0	0
32	MASALSKIS, Edgars	G	3	0	0	0	0
30	NAUMOVS, Sergejs	G	4	0	0	0	0
3	IGNATJEVS, Viktors	D	4	0	0	0	4
2	LAVINS, Rodrigo	D	4	0	0	0	4

#	In Goal	GP	Mins	GA	GAA	SO
30	NAUMOVS, Sergejs	3	180:00	10	3.33	0
1	IRBE, Arturs	1	60:00	4	4.00	0

RUSSIA

#	Name	Pos	GP	G	A	P	Pim
27	KOVALEV, Alexei	F	6	3	1	4	4
91	FEDOROV, Sergei	F	6	2	2	4	4
61	AFINOGENOV, Maxim	F	6	2	2	4	4
23	MALAKHOV, Vladimir	D	6	1	3	4	4
10	BURE, Pavel	F	6	2	1	3	8
26	DATSYUK, Pavel	F	6	1	2	3	0
14	SAMSONOV, Sergei	F	6	1	2	3	4
71	KOVALCHUK, Ilya	F	6	1	2	3	14
8	LARIONOV, Igor	F	6	0	3	3	4
7	TVERDOVSKY, Oleg	D	6	1	1	2	0
79	YASHIN, Alexei	F	6	1	1	2	0
29	KRAVCHUK, Igor	D	6	0	2	2	0
2	MIRONOV, Boris	D	6	0	1	1	2
20	BURE, Valeri	F	6	1	0	1	2
11	KASPARAITIS, Darius	D	6	0	1	1	4
13	ZHAMNOV, Alexei	F	6	1	0	1	4
5	MARKOV, Danny	D	5	0	1	1	0
33	NIKOLISHIN, Andrei	F	6	0	1	1	6
12	KVASHA, Oleg	F	5	0	0	0	0
35	KHABIBULIN, Nikolai	G	6	0	0	0	0
31	PODOMATSKI, Yegor	G	6	0	0	0	0
30	BRYZGALOV, Ilja	G	6	0	0	0	0
55	GONCHAR, Sergei	D	6	0	0	0	0

#	In Goal	GP	Mins	GA	GAA	SO
35	KHABIBULIN, Nikolai	6	359:12	14	2.34	1

SLOVAKIA

#	Name	Pos	GP	G	A	P	Pim
81	HOSSA, Marian	F	2	4	2	6	0
19	PAVLIKOVSKY, Rastislav	F	4	2	3	5	6
15	STUMPEL, Josef	F	2	2	1	3	0
24	PARDAVY, Jan	F	4	2	1	3	14
38	DEMITRA, Pavol	F	2	1	2	3	2
17	VISNOVSKY, Lubomir	D	3	1	2	3	0
41	LINTNER, Richard	D	4	1	1	2	0
39	PETROVICKY, Robert	F	4	1	1	2	2
11	MILO, Dusan	D	2	0	2	2	2
26	HANDZUS, Michal	F	2	1	0	1	6
18	SATAN, Miroslav	F	2	0	1	1	0
23	BARTECKO, Lubos	F	4	0	1	1	0
30	KAPUS, Richard	F	4	0	1	1	0
22	MAJESKY, Ivan	D	4	0	1	1	4
33	PALFFY, Zigmund	F	1	0	0	0	0
25	LASAK, Jan	G	3	0	0	0	0
31	STANA, Rastislav	G	4	0	0	0	0
29	RYBAR, Pavol	G	4	0	0	0	0
4	SMREK, Peter	D	4	0	0	0	0
72	TOROK, Jaroslav	F	4	0	0	0	0
5	OBSUT, Jaroslav	D	4	0	0	0	2
50	PAVLIKOVSKY, Richard	D	4	0	0	0	4
42	SECHNY, Richard	F	4	0	0	0	6

#	In Goal	GP	Mins	GA	GAA	SO
31	STANA, Rastislav	1	60:00	1	1.00	0
29	RYBAR, Pavol	2	84:46	5	3.54	0
25	LASAK, Jan	2	94:23	6	3.81	0

SWEDEN

#	Name	Pos	GP	G	A	P	Pim
13	SUNDIN, Mats	F	4	5	4	9	10
5	LIDSTROM, Nicklas	D	4	1	5	6	0
11	ALFREDSSON, Daniel	F	4	1	4	5	2
24	SUNDSTROM, Niklas	F	4	1	3	4	0
91	NASLUND, Markus	F	4	2	1	3	0
22	DAHLEN, Ulf	F	4	1	2	3	0
92	NYLANDER, Michael	F	4	1	2	3	0
3	JOHNSSON, Kim	D	4	1	1	2	0
10	RAGNARSSON, Marcus	D	4	0	2	2	2
2	OHLUND, Mattias	D	4	0	2	2	2
29	JONSSON, Kenny	D	3	1	0	1	2
17	JOHANSSON, Mathias	F	4	1	0	1	0
96	HOLMSTROM, Tomas	F	4	1	0	1	2
19	RENBERG, Mikael	F	4	1	0	1	4
40	ZETTERBERG, Henrik	F	4	0	1	1	0
32	TELLQVIST, Mikael	G	3	0	0	0	0
35	SALO, Tommy	G	4	0	0	0	0
1	HEDBERG, Johan	G	1	0	0	0	0
20	ARVEDSON, Magnus	F	4	0	0	0	0
14	NORSTROM, Mattias	D	4	0	0	0	0
4	OLAUSSON, Fredrik	D	4	0	0	0	2
12	AXELSSON, Per-Johan	F	4	0	0	0	2
42	JONSSON, Jorgen	F	4	0	0	0	4

#	In Goal	GP	Mins	GA	GAA	SO
1	HEDBERG, Johan	1	60:00	1	1.00	0
35	SALO, Tommy	3	179:03	7	2.35	0

SWITZERLAND

#	Name	Pos	GP	G	A	P	Pim
19	AESCHLIMANN, J.J.	F	4	3	3	6	2
18	ROTHELI, Andre	F	4	1	2	3	2
28	PLUSS, Martin	F	4	2	0	2	2
35	JEANNIN, Sandy	F	4	1	1	2	0
7	STREIT, Mark	D	4	1	1	2	0
32	RUTHEMANN, Ivo	F	4	1	1	2	0
5	SUTTER, Patrik	D	4	0	2	2	6
3	VAUCLAIR, Julien	D	4	1	0	1	2
21	FISCHER, Patrick	F	4	1	0	1	4
15	VON ARX, Reto	F	2	0	1	1	0
31	SEGER, Mathias	D	4	0	1	1	4
17	CRAMERI, Gian-Marco	F	4	0	1	1	4
22	KELLER, Olivier	D	4	0	1	1	6
4	CONNE, Flavien	F	1	0	0	0	0
27	SALIS, Edgar	D	2	0	0	0	0
30	JENNI, Marcel	F	2	0	0	0	0
26	GERBER, Martin	G	4	0	0	0	0
40	AEBISCHER, David	G	4	0	0	0	0
10	HOHENER, Martin	D	4	0	0	0	0
41	WEIBEL, Lars	G	4	0	0	0	0
12	DELLA ROSSA, Patric	F	4	0	0	0	2
11	STEINEGGER, Martin	D	4	0	0	0	6
37	CHRISTEN, Bjorn	F	4	0	0	0	6

#	In Goal	GP	Mins	GA	GAA	SO
26	GERBER, Martin	3	157:44	4	1.52	0
40	AEBISCHER, David	2	81:19	6	4.43	0

Final Statistics — Men

UKRAINE

#	Name	Pos	GP	G	A	P	Pim
16	CHIBIREV, Igor	F	4	2	1	3	2
21	OLETSKY, Valentyn	F	4	2	1	3	4
23	SALNIKOV, Roman	F	4	0	3	3	8
8	KHRISTICH, Dmitri	F	2	2	0	2	0
10	SHAKHRAYCHUK, Vadim	F	4	2	0	2	4
26	PONIKAROVSKY, Alexei	F	4	1	1	2	6
14	SHYRYAEV, Valeriy	D	4	0	2	2	0
11	FEDOTENKO, Ruslan	F	1	1	0	1	4
17	VARLAMOV, Sergei	F	2	1	0	1	14
24	SIEROV, Vladislav	F	4	0	1	1	0
25	SAVENKO, Bogdan	F	4	0	1	1	2
7	BOBROVNIKOV, Vasyl	F	4	0	1	1	2
2	GUNKO, Yuriy	D	4	0	1	1	4
15	LYTVYNENKO, Vitaliy	F	4	0	1	1	4
6	SRYUBKO, Andriy	D	4	0	1	1	6
3	KLYMENTYEV, Sergii	D	4	0	1	1	8
22	FEDOROV, Oleksandr	G	3	0	0	0	0
20	KARPENKO, Igor	G	4	0	0	0	0
1	SIMCHUK, Kostyantyn	G	4	0	0	0	0
9	SLIVCHENKO, Vadym	F	4	0	0	0	0
30	ZAVALNYUK, Vyacheslav	D	4	0	0	0	4
12	TOLKOUNOV, Dmytro	D	4	0	0	0	4
29	TIMCHENKO, Vyacheslav	D	4	0	0	0	8

#	In Goal	GP	Mins	GA	GAA	SO
1	SIMCHUK, Kostyantyn	3	174:00	9	3.10	0
20	KARPENKO, Igor	3	65:29	5	4.58	0

USA

#	Name	Pos	GP	G	A	P	Pim
16	HULL, Brett	F	6	3	5	8	6
10	LECLAIR, John	F	6	6	1	7	2
9	MODANO, Mike	F	6	0	6	6	4
6	HOUSLEY, Phil	D	6	1	4	5	0
97	ROENICK, Jeremy	F	6	1	4	5	2
2	LEETCH, Brian	D	6	0	5	5	0
48	YOUNG, Scott	F	6	4	0	4	2
13	GUERIN, Bill	F	6	4	0	4	4
11	AMONTE, Tony	F	6	2	2	4	0
3	RAFALSKI, Brian	D	6	1	2	3	2
12	ROLSTON, Brian	F	6	0	3	3	0
39	WEIGHT, Doug	F	6	0	3	3	4
7	TKACHUK, Keith	F	5	2	0	2	2
28	DEADMARSH, Adam	F	6	1	1	2	2
24	CHELIOS, Chris	D	6	1	0	1	4
61	YORK, Mike	F	6	0	1	1	0
20	SUTER, Gary	D	6	0	1	1	4
5	POTI, Tom	D	6	0	1	1	4
30	BARRASSO, Tom	G	6	0	0	0	0
35	RICHTER, Mike	G	6	0	0	0	0
1	DUNHAM, Mike	G	6	0	0	0	0
18	DRURY, Chris	F	6	0	0	0	0
33	MILLER, Aaron	D	6	0	0	0	4

#	In Goal	GP	Mins	GA	GAA	SO
1	DUNHAM, Mike	1	60:00	0	0.00	1
30	BARRASSO, Tom	1	60:00	1	1.00	0
35	RICHTER, Mike	4	240:00	9	2.25	1

Final Statistics — Women

CANADA

#	Name	Pos	GP	G	A	P	Pim
22	WICKENHEISER, Hayley	F	5	7	3	10	2
15	GOYETTE, Danielle	F	5	3	7	10	0
16	HEFFORD, Jayna	F	5	3	4	7	2
61	SUNOHARA, Vicky	F	5	4	2	6	6
17	BOTTERILL, Jennifer	F	5	3	3	6	8
13	OUELLETTE, Caroline	F	5	2	4	6	6
7	PIPER, Cherie	F	5	3	2	5	0
6	BRISSON, Therese	D	5	2	3	5	6
77	CAMPBELL, Cassie	F	5	2	1	3	2
73	CHARTRAND, Isabelle	D	5	2	1	3	2
23	ANTAL, Dana	F	5	2	1	3	2
25	SHEWCHUK, Tammy Lee	F	5	1	1	2	0
12	DUPUIS, Lori	F	5	1	1	2	4
91	HEANEY, Geraldine	D	5	0	2	2	0
5	SOSTORICS, Colleen	D	5	0	2	2	4
33	ST. PIERRE, Kim	G	5	0	1	1	0
24	BECHARD, Kelly	F	5	0	1	1	2
4	KELLAR, Becky	D	5	0	1	1	6
11	POUNDER, Cheryl	D	5	0	0	0	0
1	SMALL, Sami Jo	G	5	0	0	0	0

#	In Goal	GP	Mins	GA	GAA	SO
1	SMALL, Sami Jo	1	60:00	0	0.00	1
33	ST. PIERRE, Kim	4	240:00	5	1.25	2

CHINA

#	Name	Pos	GP	G	A	P	Pim
3	LIU, Hongmei	F	5	3	1	4	4
8	YANG, Xiuqing	F	5	3	1	4	14
14	SUN, Rui	F	5	2	2	4	2
11	HU, Chunrong	F	5	0	3	3	4
19	WANG, Linuo	F	5	0	2	2	4
18	MA, Xiaojun	F	5	1	0	1	2
10	CHEN, Jing	D	5	0	1	1	4
12	JIN, Fengling	F	5	0	1	1	4
13	ZHANG, Jing	F	5	0	0	0	0
1	JIANG, Limei	F	5	0	0	0	0
21	GUAN, Weinan	D	5	0	0	0	0
24	SHEN, Tiantian	D	5	0	0	0	0
22	DAI, Qiuwa	F	5	0	0	0	0
4	LI, Xuan	D	5	0	0	0	2
2	WANG, Ying	D	5	0	0	0	2
20	GUO, Hong	G	5	0	0	0	4
6	LU, Yan	D	5	0	0	0	4
9	SANG, Hong	D	5	0	0	0	4
7	XU, Lei	D	5	0	0	0	6
15	LIU, Yanhui	F	5	0	0	0	6

#	In Goal	GP	Mins	GA	GAA	SO
20	GUO, Hong	5	301:39	26	5.17	0

Final Statistics — Women

FINLAND

#	Name	Pos	GP	G	A	P	Pim
28	RIIPI, Katja	F	5	3	3	6	6
16	REIMA, Tiia	F	5	2	1	3	2
20	HANNINEN, Kirsi	D	5	0	3	3	0
10	FISK, Sari	F	5	0	3	3	0
13	NIEMINEN, Riikka	F	5	0	3	3	2
23	SIKIO, Hanne	F	5	2	0	2	2
3	LAAKSONEN, Emma	D	5	1	1	2	2
6	SIRVIO, Saija	D	5	1	1	2	10
29	RANTAMAKI, Karoliina	F	5	1	0	1	0
11	PARVIAINEN, Oona	F	5	1	0	1	0
8	VOUTILAINEN, Marjo	F	5	0	1	1	2
15	HOIKKALA, Satu	F	5	0	1	1	2
9	MERTANEN, Terhi	D	5	0	1	1	2
19	PUPUTTI, Tuula	G	5	0	0	0	0
30	HALONEN, Minna-Monica	G	5	0	0	0	0
25	PALVILA, Marja-Helena	F	5	0	0	0	2
5	AHONEN, Pirjo	D	5	0	0	0	2
26	SAVIKUJA, Henna	F	5	0	0	0	4
22	SALO, Paivi	D	5	0	0	0	12
21	VAARAKALLIO, Petra	F	5	0	0	0	16

#	In Goal	GP	Mins	GA	GAA	SO
19	PUPUTTI, Tuula	5	299:22	15	3.01	1

GERMANY

#	Name	Pos	GP	G	A	P	Pim
81	BECKER, Maritta	F	5	3	2	5	8
21	LANZL, Michaela	F	5	3	1	4	6
19	OSWALD, Christine	F	5	1	2	3	4
25	RUCKAUER, Sabine	D	5	0	2	2	2
8	ZIEGENHALS, Nina	D	5	0	2	2	2
15	RITTER, Nina	F	5	1	0	1	0
71	WIERSCHER, Julia	F	5	1	0	1	0
29	GRUNDMANN, Claudia	F	5	1	0	1	2
13	WARTOSCH-KURTEN, Stephanie	G	5	0	1	1	0
20	LINDE, Nina	D	5	0	1	1	0
14	SCHEYTT, Anja	F	5	0	1	1	0
54	VALENTI, Maren	F	5	0	1	1	2
9	WOLF, Raffi	F	5	0	1	1	4
24	FRUHWIRT, Stephanie	F	5	0	1	1	6
22	THYSSEN, Esther	G	5	0	0	0	0
66	EVERS, Bettina	F	5	0	0	0	0
69	KINZA, Sandra	D	5	0	0	0	2
17	REINDL, Franziska	F	5	0	0	0	2
23	KRUCK, Sabrina	D	5	0	0	0	6
44	SCHRECKENBACH, Jana	D	5	0	0	0	8

#	In Goal	GP	Mins	GA	GAA	SO
13	WARTOSCH-KURTEN, Stephanie	5	228:53	14	3.67	1
22	THYSSEN, Esther	2	71:07	9	7.59	0

KAZAKHSTAN

#	Name	Pos	GP	G	A	P	Pim
19	YAKOVCHUK, Natalya	F	5	1	0	1	0
11	LOSYEVA, Nadezhda	F	5	1	0	1	2
21	SAZONOVA, Viktorya	D	5	0	1	1	0
9	POTAPOVA, Olga	D	5	0	1	1	4
29	VASSINA, Svetlana	F	5	0	1	1	6
33	TRUNOVA, Natalya	G	5	0	0	0	0
1	AKIMBETYEVA, Anna	G	5	0	0	0	0
27	MALTSEVA, Svetlana	F	5	0	0	0	0
7	ALEXEYEVA, Lyubov	F	5	0	0	0	0
16	KONYSHEVA, Olga	F	5	0	0	0	0
23	MALTSEVA, Yekaterina	F	5	0	0	0	2
10	SHTELMAISTER, Yelena	F	5	0	0	0	2
6	VAFINA, Lyubov	F	5	0	0	0	2
5	KHLYZOVA, Tatyana	F	5	0	0	0	2
2	ASSONOVA, Antonida	D	5	0	0	0	4
30	SOLOVYEVA, Yuliya	F	5	0	0	0	4
12	ADYYEVA, Viktorya	D	5	0	0	0	6
14	DIKAMBAYEVA, Dinara	F	5	0	0	0	6
17	KRYUKOVA, Olga	D	5	0	0	0	14
4	TAIKEVICH, Oxana	D	5	0	0	0	16

#	In Goal	GP	Mins	GA	GAA	SO
33	TRUNOVA, Natalya	5	301:39	24	4.77	0

RUSSIA

#	Name	Pos	GP	G	A	P	Pim
25	PACHKEVITCH, Ekaterina	F	5	3	2	5	2
23	BURINA, Tatiana	F	5	4	0	4	0
17	SMOLENTSEVA, Ekaterina	F	5	1	3	4	6
18	TSAREVA, Tatiana	F	5	3	0	3	18
21	TREFILOVA, Svetlana	F	5	1	2	3	6
29	SHCHELCHKOVA, Zhanna	D	5	0	3	3	2
10	MISHINA, Larisa	F	5	2	0	2	0
7	BOBROVA, Elena	D	5	0	2	2	4
22	TERENTIEVA, Svetlana	F	5	1	0	1	2
27	BIALKOVSKAIA, Elena	F	5	0	1	1	0
15	PERMYAKOVA, Olga	D	5	0	1	1	6
20	GACHENNIKOVA, Irina	G	5	0	0	0	0
4	KHOMITCH, Alena	D	5	0	0	0	0
3	PETROVSKAIA, Kristina	D	5	0	0	0	0
11	SOTNIKOVA, Tatiana	F	5	0	0	0	0
30	VOTINTSEVA, Irina	G	5	0	0	0	0
12	GLADYSHEVA, Ioulia	F	5	0	0	0	2
2	BARYKINA, Maria	D	5	0	0	0	4
28	TRETIAKOVA, Oksana	F	5	0	0	0	4
26	SAVENKOVA, Olga	D	5	0	0	0	12

#	In Goal	GP	Mins	GA	GAA	SO
20	GASHENNIKOVA, Irina	5	300:00	12	2.40	1

SWEDEN

#	Name	Pos	GP	G	A	P	Pim
8	HOLST, Erika	F	5	2	3	5	10
7	ROTH, Maria	F	5	1	3	4	10
14	BERGSTRAND, Kristina	F	5	2	1	3	2
19	ALMBLAD, Lotta	F	4	2	0	2	0
10	SAMUELSSON, Evelina	F	5	2	0	2	0
23	ANDERSSON, Gunilla	D	5	1	1	2	12
9	VIKMAN, Anna	F	5	1	0	1	0
17	EDSTRAND, Ann-Louise	D	5	1	0	1	2
18	PETTERSSON, Josefin	F	5	0	1	1	2
27	LINDBERG, Ylva	D	5	0	1	1	4
6	ANDERSSON, Anna	D	5	0	1	1	8
30	MARTIN, Kim	G	5	0	0	0	0
11	LARSSON, Maria	F	5	0	0	0	0
35	AHLEN, Annica	G	5	0	0	0	2
29	LINDSTROM, Ulrica	F	5	0	0	0	2
24	JANSSON, Nanna	F	5	0	0	0	2
28	RUNDQVIST, Danijela	F	5	0	0	0	2
5	BERGGREN, Emelie	D	5	0	0	0	2
25	SJOLANDER, Therese	D	5	0	0	0	6
21	ELFSBERG, Joa	F	5	0	0	0	6

#	In Goal	GP	Mins	GA	GAA	SO
30	MARTIN, Kim	3	180:00	5	1.67	1
35	AHLEN, Annika	2	120:00	13	6.50	0

USA

#	Name	Pos	GP	G	A	P	Pim
21	GRANATO, Cammi	F	5	6	4	10	0
22	DARWITZ, Natalie	F	5	7	1	8	2
20	KING, Katie	F	5	4	3	7	4
12	POTTER, Jenny	F	5	1	6	7	2
2	MOUNSEY, Tara	D	5	0	7	7	4
6	BYE, Karyn	F	5	3	3	6	0
17	WENDELL, Krissy	F	5	1	5	6	6
8	BAKER, Laurie	F	5	3	2	5	4
13	CHU, Julie	F	5	2	2	4	2
11	MLECZKO, A.J	D	5	1	3	4	6
4	RUGGIERO, Angela	D	5	1	3	4	8
24	BAILEY, Chris	D	5	1	2	3	0
15	LOONEY, Shelley	F	5	1	2	3	2
9	KILBOURNE, Andrea	F	5	1	1	2	2
3	KENNEDY, Courtney	D	5	0	2	2	6
14	MERZ, Sue	D	4	1	0	1	0
1	DECOSTA, Sara	G	5	0	1	1	0
5	WALL, Lyndsay	D	5	0	1	1	4
29	TUETING, Sarah	G	5	0	0	0	0
25	DUNN, Tricia	F	5	0	0	0	29

#	In Goal	GP	Mins	GA	GAA	SO
29	TUETING, Sarah	2	120:00	1	0.50	1
1	DECOSTA, Sara	3	180:00	3	1.00	2

1920
TEAM CANADA: Winnipeg Falcons

Wally Byron, goalie
Bobby Benson, defence
Konnie Johannesson, defence
Frank Fredrickson, centre (captain)
Chris Fridfinnson, forward
Magnus "Mike" Goodman, left wing
Halldor "Slim" Halderson, right wing
Allan "Huck" Woodman, rover

Herbert "Hebby". Axford, coach
Bill Fridfinsson, secretary
William Hewitt, manager
Gordon Sigurjonson, trainer

1924
TEAM CANADA: Toronto Granites

Jack Cameron, goal
Ernie Collett, goal
Dunc Munro, defence (captain)
Beattie Ramsay, defence
Hooley Smith, centre
Cyril "Sig" Slater, left wing
Harry Watson, left wing
Bert McCaffery, right wing
Harold McMunn, right wing

Frank Rankin, coach
William Hewitt, general manager

1928
TEAM CANADA: University of Toronto Graduates

Norbert "Stuffy" Mueller, goalie
Dr. Joe Sullivan, goalie
Frank Fisher, defence
Rogers "Rod" Plaxton, defence
John "Red" Porter, defence (captain)
Ross Taylor, defence
Dr. Lou Hudson, right wing
Dave Trottier, left wing
Hugh Plaxton, centre
Charlie Delahey, forward
Bert Plaxton, forward
Grant Gordon, forward
Frank Sullivan, forward

Conn Smythe, coach
William Hewitt, manager

1932
TEAM CANADA: The Winnipegs

William Cockburn, goal (captain)
Stanley Wagner, goal
Roy Hinkel, defence
Hugh Sutherland, defence
George Garbutt, centre
Walter Monson, centre
Harold "Hack" Simpson, centre
Bert "Spunk" Duncanson, left wing
Romeo Rivers, left wing
Aliston "Stoney" Wise, left wing
Clifford Crowley, right wing
Victor Lindquist, right wing
Norm Malloy, right wing
Kenneth Moore, right wing

Jack Hughes, coach
Lou Marsh, manager

1936
TEAM CANADA: Port Arthur Bear Cats

Francis "Dinty" Moore, goal
Arthur "Jakie" Nash, goal
Walter "Pud" Kitchen, defence
Ray Milton, defence
Herman Murray, defence (captain)
Hugh Farquharson, centre
Alexander Sinclair, centre
Maxwell "Bill" Deacon, left wing
Ralph St. Germain, left wing
Dave Neville, right wing
Bill Thomson, right wing
Ken Farmer, forward
Jim Haggarty, forward

Al Pudas, coach
Malcolm Cochrane, manager

1948
TEAM CANADA: Royal Canadian Air Force (RCAF) Flyers

Aircraftsman 2 Murray Dowey, goal
Flying Officer Frank Dunster, defence
Aircraftsman 2 Andre Laperriere, defence
Flight Sergeant Louis Lecompte, defence
Aircraftsman 1 Orval Gravelle, forward
Corporal Patrick "Patsy" Guzzo, forward
Wally Halder (civilian), forward
Aircraftsman 1 Ted "Red" Hibberd, forward
George Mara (civilian), forward (captain)
Leading Aircraftsman Ab Renaud, forward
Flying Officer Reg Schroeter, forward
Corporal Irving Taylor, forward

Sergeant Frank Boucher, coach
Squadron Leader A. Gardner "Sandy"
Watson, manager

1952
TEAM CANADA: Edmonton Mercurys

Ralph Hansch, goal
Eric Patterson, goal
John Davies, defence
Don Gauf, defence
Bob Meyers, defence
Tom Pollock, defence
Al Purvis, defence
George Abel, forward
Billy Dawe, forward (captain)
Bruce Dickson, forward
Billy Gibson, centre
David Miller, left wing
Gordie Robertson, forward
Louis Secco, forward
Frank "Sully" Sullivan, forward
Robert Watt, forward

Lou Holmes, coach
Jim Christianson, manager

1956
TEAM CANADA: Kitchener-Waterloo Dutchmen

Denis Brodeur, goal
Keith Woodall, goal
Art Hurst, defence
Byrle Klinck, defence
Howie Lee, defence
Jack MacKenzie, defence (captain)
Floyd Martin, defence
Billy Colvin, centre
Ken Laufman, centre
Bob White, centre
Charlie Brooker, left wing
Jim Logan, left wing
Don Rope, left wing
Gerry Theberge, left wing
Buddy Horne, right wing
Paul Knox, right wing
George Scholes, right wing

Bobby Bauer, coach
Ernie Gorman, general manager

1960
TEAM CANADA: Kitchener-Waterloo Dutchmen

Don Head, goal
Harold "Boat" Hurley, goal
Moe Benoit, defence
Jack Douglas, defence
Harry Sinden, defence (captain)
Darryl Sly, defence
Bob Attersley, forward
Jim Connelly, forward
Fred Etcher, forward
Bob Forhan, forward
Ken Laufman, forward
Floyd "Butch" Martin, forward
Bob McKnight, forward
Cliff Pennington, forward
Don Rope, forward
Bobby Rousseau, forward
George Samolenko, forward

Bobby Bauer, coach
Ernie Gorman, general manager

1964
TEAM CANADA

Ken Broderick, goal
Seth Martin, goal
Hank Akervall, defence (captain)
Barry MacKenzie, defence
Terry O'Malley, defence
Rod Seiling, defence
Gary Begg, centre
Gary Dineen, centre
George Swarbrick, centre
Roger Bourbonnais, left wing
Terry Clancy, left wing
Brian Conacher, left wing
Ray Cadieux, right wing
Paul Conlin, right wing
Bob Forhan, right wing
Marshall Johnston, right wing

Father David Bauer, coach
Dr. Bob Hindmarch, manager

1968
TEAM CANADA

Ken Broderick, goal
Wayne Stephenson, goal
Paul Conlin, defence
Brian Glennie, defence
Ted Hargreaves, defence
Marshall Johnston, defence (captain)
Barry MacKenzie, defence
Terry O'Malley, defence
Roger Bourbonnais, forward
Ray Cadieux, forward
Gary Dineen, forward
Fran Huck, forward
Billy MacMillan, forward
Steve Monteith, forward
Morris Mott, forward
Danny O'Shea, forward
Gerry Pinder, forward
Herb Pinder, forward

Jackie McLeod, coach
Father David Bauer, manager

1972 & 1976 did not compete

1980
TEAM CANADA

Bob Dupuis, goal
Paul Pageau, goal
Warren Anderson, defence
Joe Grant, defence
Randy Gregg, defence (captain)
Terry O'Malley, defence
Brad Pirie, defence
Don Spring, defence
Tim Watters, defence
Glenn Anderson, forward
Ken Berry, forward
Dan D'Alvise, forward
Ron Davidson, forward
John Devaney, forward
Dave Hindmarch, forward
Paul MacLean, forward
Kevin Maxwell, forward
Jim Nill, forward
Kevin Primeau, forward
Stelio Zupancich, forward

Lorne Davis, co-coach
Clare Drake, co-coach
Tom Watt, co-coach
Rick Noonan, manager
Father David Bauer, managing director

1984
TEAM CANADA

Darren Eliot, goal
Mario Gosselin, goal
Warren Anderson, defence
Robin Bartel, defence
J.J. Daigneault, defence
Bruce Driver, defence
Doug Lidster, defence
James Patrick, defence
Craig Redmond, defence
Russ Courtnall, forward
Kevin Dineen, forward
Dave Donnelly, forward
Pat Flatley, forward
Dave Gagner, forward
Vaughn Karpan, forward
Darren Lowe, forward
Kirk Muller, forward
Dave Tippett, forward (captain)
Carey Wilson, forward
Dan Wood, forward

Dave King, coach & general manager
George Kingston, assistant coach
Jean Perron, assistant coach

1988
TEAM CANADA

Sean Burke, goal
Andy Moog, goal
Chris Felix, defence
Randy Gregg, defence
Serge Roy, defence
Tony Stiles, defence
Tim Watters, defence
Trent Yawney, defence
Zarley Zalapski, defence
Ken Berry, centre
Mark Habscheid, centre
Vaughn Karpan, left wing
Wally Schreiber, left wing
Gord Sherven, right wing
Claude Vilgrain, right wing
Serge Boisvert, forward
Brian Bradley, forward
Bob Joyce, forward
Merlin Malinowski, forward
Jim Peplinski, forward
Steve Tambellini, forward
Ken Yaremchuk, forward

Dave King, coach & general manager
Guy Charron, assistant coach
Tom Watt, assistant coach

1992
TEAM CANADA

Sean Burke, goal
Trevor Kidd, goal
Kevin Dahl, defence
Curt Giles, defence
Gord Hynes, defence
Adrien Plavsic, defence
Dan Ratushny, defence
Brad Schlegel, defence (captain)
Brian Tutt, defence
Jason Woolley, defence
Dave Archibald, forward
Todd Brost, forward
Dave Hannan, forward
Fabian Joseph, forward
Joe Juneau, forward
Patrick Lebeau, forward
Chris Lindberg, forward
Eric Lindros, forward
Kent Manderville, forward
Wally Schreiber, forward
Randy Smith, forward
Dave Tippett, forward

Dave King, coach and general manager
Terry Crisp, assistant coach
Wayne Fleming, assistant coach

1994
TEAM CANADA

Corey Hirsch, goal
Mark Astley, defence
Adrian Aucoin, defence
David Harlock, defence
Ken Lovsin, defence
Derek Mayer, defence
Brad Schlegel, defence
Chris Therien, defence
Brad Werenka, defence
Greg Johnson, centre
Petr Nedved, centre
Greg Parks, centre
Todd Warriner, centre
Fabian Joseph, left wing
Paul Kariya, left wing
Jean-Yves Roy, left wing
Wally Schreiber, left wing
Todd Hlushko, right wing
Chris Kontos, right wing
Dwayne Norris, right wing
Brian Savage, right wing

Tom Renney, coach
Danny Dube, associate coach
George Kingston, Director of Hockey Operations

1998
TEAM CANADA

Patrick Roy, goal
Rob Blake, defence
Eric Desjardins, defence
Adam Foote, defence
Al MacInnis, defence
Ray Bourque, defence
Chris Pronger, defence
Scott Stevens, defence
Rob Zamuner, forward
Mark Recchi, forward
Brendan Shanahan, forward
Trevor Linden, forward
Steve Yzerman, forward
Rob Brind'Amour, forward
Joe Nieuwendyk, forward
Sjayne Corson, forward
Theoren Fleury, forward
Keith Primeau, forward
Wayne Gretzky, forward
Eric Lindros, forward
Joe Sakic, forward

Marc Crawford, head coach

1998
Women's Team

Lesley Reddon, goal
Manon Rheaume, goal
Becky Kellar, defence
Therese Brisson, defence
Fiona Smith, defence
Judy Diduck, defence
Cassie Campbell, defence
Geraldine Heaney, defence
France St. Louis, forward
Jennifer Botterill, forward
Lori Dupuis, forward
Katheryn McCormack, forward
Danielle Goyette, forward
Jayna Hefford, forward
Stacy Wilson, forward
Nancy Drolet, forward
Hayley Wickenheiser, forward
Laura Schuler, forward
Vicky Sunohara, forward
Karen Nystrom, forward

1952 EDMONTON MERCURYS-CANADA'S LAST GOLD

The Mercurys' selection by the CAHA to represent Canada the 1952 Games differed slightly in rationale from the usual process of simply penning in the name of the Allan Cup champions. While teams from the west were still considered the best in Canada in 1951, the Western Senior A league had gone from being an amateur congregation in 1950 to semi-pro in 1951, thus disqualifying most of the teams and players from Olympic eligibility. The Mercurys, an Intermediate club, were still highly regarded and through both their performance on ice and their clean record as amateurs they were invited to represent Canada in Oslo.

The Mercurys got to Europe early in the new year and stayed well after the Games were over, playing an extensive series of exhibition games throughout the Continent, at first to prepare themselves for the competition and then to promote their excellent skills and high standards of play and delight fans unused to seeing such a calibre of hockey.

This was the first time a Canadian team travelled to the Games by plane, leaving from Montreal and arriving at Prestwick, Scotland on January 5, 1952. There, bedecked in white Stetsons, the Mercs were greeted by W. Duncan, president of the Scottish Ice Hockey Association, and Ross Low, manager of Ayr Arena. Less than an hour later, the Canadian boys were on the ice playing their first exhibition game, a 6-3 win over the Ayr Raiders. They played two more games in Scotland, then a series in London, and carried on to the Continent for more Olympic tune-ups.

The team was backed financially by Jim Christianson of Edmonton, a car dealer who provided the $100,000 needed to tour Europe and participate in the Olympics, and who, as owner, named the team after a brand of Fords he frequently sold. Christianson was in many ways a remarkable man and great hockey fan. He revived the Junior Oil Kings franchise which went on to win a Memorial Cup, and as owner of one of the most successful Lincoln Mercury dealerships in the country, his business acumen was indisputable.

While in Norway with the team, he contracted a virus and was ill for most of the Games. Upon his return to Canada, he again became ill and died a short time later. The Ford Motor Company then appointed a dealer principal who oversaw operations for the next decade or so, and when he died, Mercs defenceman Al Purvis was named the next dealer principal. Purvis then got a number of his Olympics teammates on board as shareholders (Miller, Gauf, and Dawe) or employees, each managing a division of the operations. Over the years, he bought back their shares, and to this day Al Purvis runs the Waterloo Mercury dealership in Edmonton, now celebrating 50 years of operation

The European tour was immensely successful for the Mercurys. Everywhere they went, they amazed fans who had never seen such speed and strength coupled with unparalleled skill. And everywhere the Mercs went, they won. They played in the great outdoor Jordal Amfi stadium in Oslo, where 10,000 fans watched the Canucks beat the Norwegian aggregation 7-2 in an exhibition on the site where most of the Olympic games would be played (along with nearby Daalenenga Stadium, another outdoor rink).

Halfway through the Games, the gold medal team of 1948 sent a cable to the team trying to continue the Olympic reign: "Former members RCAF Flyers, 1948 Winter Olympic champs and all of RCAF, pulling for Mercs. Confident you will bring home Olympic title. Good luck and best wishes."

The Canada-Czech game and the USA-Swiss game were thrown into a very bad light when reporters focused on two non-fights instigated by a Canadian and an American, respectively. Both Gordie Robertson of Canada and, more seriously, Joe Czarnota of the States received major penalties for waving at an opponent, but Zurich's leading paper, *Neue Zuricher Zeitung*, was outraged, commenting: "We have neither the words nor the space to describe in detail what some of these rowdies drilled in circus business considered permissible. It is now time to ask

whether this pollution of European ice hockey through overseas teams should not be halted. One can be certain that neither the Canadians nor the Americans would let themselves be criticized. However, what seems good enough for their players and their public need not be held up as a model for European circumstances." The editorial concluded by questioning "whether an ice hockey tournament under such unfavourable auspices might not better be stricken from the Olympic program."

When asked to comment, Norway's Prime Minister Oscar Torp defended the brand of hockey on display: "Just ignorance of the mainly-Norwegian crowd," he concluded. "People should understand that the penalties make ice hockey a human game. When the boys get so het up that they do something wrong or get too rowdy — OK, give them two minutes to cool down and think it over. Ice hockey is a terrific display, not only of teamwork but also of technique and bodily strength. So, of course, the lads will hurt each other now and then."

The next day, after an hour's meeting by the IIHF, under the directorship of Dr. Fritz Kraatz, the fire was doused. No suspensions were levied and the games went on as planned.

After winning gold, the Mercurys

travelled through Belgium, Holland, Sweden, Norway, Switzerland, Italy, and England again. All in all, they won 45 of the 50 games they played, the last a 7-2 win over the Earl's Court Rangers, before flying home April 1, 1952.

Canada had been so far the superior hockey-playing nation in the world since 1920, and part of our teams' mandate had always been to tour Europe in good faith to promote hockey, Canada, and Canadian skills. In return, the players were culturally enriched by the time spent in these countries and certainly enjoyed the games. However, they received no remuneration beyond living expenses (they were, after all, amateurs) and, worse, were frequently berated, most often during tense games at the Olympics, for incorporating too much the physical side of the game into play. This criticism exasperated the CAHA, which felt increasingly that travelling teams had little to gain and much to lose.

Thus, the following year, the feeling was that Canada should not send a touring team to the World Championships in Switzerland, a decision made officially by CAHA president W.B. George but one fully supported by everybody. As George rationalized: "Every year we spend $10,000 to send a Canadian hockey team over to Europe to play 40 exhibition games. All of these games are played to packed houses that only enrich European coffers. In return, we are subjected to constant, unnecessary abuse over our Canadian style of play."

Outgoing CAHA president Doug Grimston issued a caveat for Canadians after watching the swift development of teams during the course of the Oslo Games: "European teams have improved considerably the last few years and, with some proper coaching, could be mighty troublesome to Canada." He went on to observe that, "European teams lack stamina, especially on power plays, and they are timid when it comes to bodily contact." But, he warned, if these problems could be eradicated, many countries could become superior hockey-playing nations. By the time the next Olympics arrived, his words had proved timely and prescient, and it would be fully a half century to the day before Canada's men struck Olympic gold again.

ACKNOWLEDGEMENTS

The author would like to thank a number of important people for helping
get this book set in record time. Firstly, Lukas Aykroyd, Angus Gillespie,
and Kevin Shea for helping with the writing of the game reports
and profiles. Their expedience and assistance were invaluable.
To everyone at the IIHF and Hockey Hall of Fame for their support and swift
work to make the book a reality. At the IIHF: Kimmo Leinonen,
Jan-Ake Edvinsson, Dave Fitzpatrick, Rene Fasel, Szymon Szemberg,
Darren Boyko, Luzia Zuber, Rob van Rijswijk, Hannes Ederer, Gion Veraguth,
Eslie Dall'Oglio, Martin Zoellner, Isabella Burgi, Federico Saviozzi, Johanna May,
and Simone Tiefenauer. At the HHOF: Phil Pritchard, Tyler Wolosewich,
Craig Campbell, Jeff Denomme, Craig Baines, Bill Hay, Kelly Masse, Pearl Rajwanth,
Carmil Guspie, Ray Paquet, Sylvia Lau, Jan Barrina, Jason Fowler, Ron Ellis,
Sandra Buffone, Jackie Boughazale, Craig Beckim, Mike Bolt, Steve Ozimec,
Tony Da Rosa, Tome Geneski, Dave Stubbs, Jo-Anne Gracie, Izak Westgate,
Mike Bolt, Peter Jagla, Stephen Ward, Geoff Fletcher, Anthony Fusco,
Margaret Lockhart, and Marilyn Robbins. Also, a special thanks to
Stephanie Hicks, whose help was much needed and appreciated.
To everyone at the media sub-centre in Salt Lake who did such a great job in
helping me gather information at every step of the way, notably Erich Bacher
and Julie Young. To everyone at Fenn, especially Jordan Fenn and
Kathryn Del Borrello, for embracing the project so thoroughly and swiftly
without wanting to sacrifice quality for speed. To Georgina McIntyre's expeditious
design and setting of the pages. To my agent Dean Cooke and to editor Eva Black.
To the members of the Canadian ice crew at the E-Center in Salt Lake,
for putting the hallowed loonie in centre ice. And, of course, to the men's
and women's national teams, for bringing home gold and reasserting Canada's
position as the greatest hockey-playing nation on the planet.

PHOTO CREDITS

Dave Sandford/Hockey Hall of Fame
pp. 6, 9, 10, 16, 17, 19, 21-23, 26-33, 35-38, 41-50, 52-61, 64, 66-133

Gerry Thomas/IIHF
pp. 11-15, 20, 25, 34, 39, 40, 51, 62, 63, 65

Matthew Manor/HHOF
p. 7

Hockey Hall of Fame Archives
p. 143